Advanced
Scratch
Programming

Abhay B. Joshi

*To my Scratch students
who inspire me to learn*

. . . .

Published by

Tanuja A. Joshi
3554 - 173rd CT NE
Redmond, WA 98052
USA
15 August 2016

To order your copy:

Go to Amazon.com
Or write to: abjoshi@yahoo.com

. . . .

Cover design and book layout by
Ravindra Pande

Introduction

Background

The idea of using *computer programming as a medium for learning* was first proposed by Seymour Papert in his ground-breaking book "Mindstorms" back in the 1980s. Dr. Papert also designed the Logo programming language specifically for this purpose. For a variety of reasons this idea remained an esoteric one and did not become mainstream until almost the turn of the century. The last decade and half has seen a dramatic change in this situation. Today, no one questions the idea anymore. The benefits of learning programming and *computer science* concepts well before college are well-understood. Everyone from the President of the United States to CEOs of major tech companies to school administrators are talking about teaching *computational thinking* to children and young adults. The focus is now on *how* to implement this idea in schools.

Here is a list of some of the amazing things that happen when children engage in computer programming:

- Children become *active* and *creative* learners, because they explore ideas through a hands-on activity with an infinitely powerful tool.
- They learn to think about and analyze *their own thinking*, because that is the only way to program computers.
- They learn to solve complex problems by breaking them down into smaller sub-problems.
- They learn a new way of thinking (called "computational" thinking).
- In the world of programming, answers are not simply "right" or "wrong"; this prepares a child's mindset for real-life problems.
- Children's learning processes are transformed from *acquiring facts* to *thinking creatively and analytically.*

There are several books and papers on this subject of "computational thinking for children and young adults". If you would like to get a quick overview of this subject, please check out my 2-page handout at:
http://scratched.gse.harvard.edu/resources/handout-learning-through-programming

About this interactive book

The choice of programming language is critical to achieve the intended objectives of teaching CS to beginners. In this book we use the Scratch programming language. Scratch is an entertaining and powerful language, and yet it is easy to learn. It is known as a "low floor and high ceiling" language – it allows the learner to build his/her vocabulary without getting mired in the complexities of syntax and grammar.

There is a lot of material on Scratch Programming on the Internet, including videos, online courses, Scratch projects, and so on, but, most of it is introductory. There is very little that can take students to the next level, where they can apply their Scratch and CS concepts to exciting and challenging problems. There is also very little material that shows students how to *design* complex projects, and introduces them to the *process* of programming.

This book is meant to fill these gaps.

In short:
- This book is for students who are already familiar with Scratch – its various commands, and its user interface – and basic CS concepts such as, variables, conditional statements, looping, and so on.
- The book attempts to teach students how to "design" programs through a series of challenging and interesting projects on science simulation, games, puzzles, and math problems.
- The book is intended for middle school children and above.

I call this an "interactive book" because it is something between a traditional book – which is static and passive – and a fully interactive online course. It does look like a book: it has a series of chapters, diagrams, a lot of text, etc. But it also contains links to online Scratch programs, code snippets, references, which the reader is expected to click and explore to fully benefit from the ideas presented.

Where to learn the CS concepts

The projects covered in this book are all based on a variety of CS and Scratch concepts. This book does not attempt to explain these concepts. If you are a newcomer to Scratch and/or CS, I recommend to you my other book **Learn CS Concepts with Scratch**. I have also prepared a supplement that provides a brief description of each of these concepts. This supplement is available for a free download at:

http://www.abhayjoshi.net/scratch/book1/supplement.pdf

What is in the book?

I have organized the book as a series of independent Scratch projects – each of which describes how to design and build an interesting and challenging Scratch program. Each project progresses in stages – from a simple implementation to increasingly complex versions. You can take up these projects in any order you like, although I have tried to arrange them in an increasing order of challenge.

Programming is a powerful tool that can be applied to virtually any field of human endeavor. I have tried to maintain a good diversity of applications in this book. You will find the following types of projects:

- Simple ball games
- Puzzle games
- Memory games
- Science simulations
- Math games
- Geometric designs

Learn the concepts through application

As the experts will tell you, concepts are really understood and internalized when you apply them to solve problems. The purpose of this book is to help you *apply* Scratch and CS concepts to solve interesting and challenging programming problems. Every chapter lists, at the very start, the Scratch and CS concepts that you will apply while building that project.

Learn the design process

Besides these technical concepts, you will also learn the "divide and conquer" approach of problem-solving. This is a fancy term for the technique of breaking down a bigger problem into many smaller problems and solving them separately one by one.
You will also learn the "iterative design process" for designing programs. This is another fancy name that describes the idea that something complex can be designed in

a repeated *idea -> implement -> test* cycle, such that in each cycle we add a little more complexity.

Finally, you will also learn a bit of "project management". Project management helps you undertake a project – such as painting your house, celebrating your sister's birthday, or creating a complex computer program – and complete it in a reasonable time, with reasonable effort, and with reasonable quality. It involves things such as planning tasks, tracking their progress, etc. When you undertake the programming projects in this book, you will learn some of these project management techniques.

Audience for the book

The book is intended for students who are already familiar with Scratch. The level of challenge is tuned for middle- and high-school students, but elementary-school students who have picked up all the concepts in an introductory course might also be able to enjoy the projects presented in this book.

The book would be a great resource for teachers who teach Scratch programming. They could use the projects to teach advanced tricks of programming and to show how complex programs are designed.

Finally, the book is for anyone who wants to get the wonderful taste of the entertaining and creative aspect of Computer Programming.

Hardware and software

To write programs described in this book you will need Scratch 2.0. There is an online version of Scratch 2.0 at http://scratch.mit.edu which you could use. You could also download the offline version of Scratch 2.0 available at https://scratch.mit.edu/scratch2download/. The offline Scratch editor works on most Windows, Mac, and Linux platforms.

Abhay B. Joshi (abjoshi@yahoo.com)
Seattle, USA
15 August 2016

Acknowledgements

The idea of writing this book came from my teaching experience of the last several years. I would like to thank Aksharnandan School in Pune for allowing me to teach Scratch to their 7th and 8th grade students every year (since 2008) during my summer visits to Pune. I am also grateful to my numerous middle and high school students with whom I worked in person or on Skype.

I owe the book to my 800+ students. They tolerated my ideas, contributed a lot of their own, and frankly told me what was interesting and what wasn't. Their programming projects were amazingly creative – which only reinforced my interest in teaching programming.

I wish to thank Tanuja Joshi for reviewing the material of this book diligently and tirelessly and for providing me with valuable suggestions. I wish to thank Ravindra Pande for formatting the chapters and for designing a truly beautiful cover for this book. Finally, this book would not have been possible without the constant encouragement of my friends and family.

I do hope that the readers will find this book useful and enjoyable.

Abhay B. Joshi (abjoshi@yahoo.com)
Seattle, USA
15 August 2016

Author's Background

As a CS teacher (since 2008), Abhay's area of interest has been teaching "Computer Programming as a medium for learning" and he has been teaching Scratch regularly to elementary, middle, and high school students in Redmond and Bellevue, WA. He also provides instruction on Skype. Abhay has been teaching 7th and 8th grade students at Aksharnandan School in Pune, India every summer since 2008. Abhay has published an introductory book on Scratch titled **Learn CS Concepts with Scratch**. Earlier in 2011 Abhay co-authored (with Sandesh Gaikwad) two books on **Logo Programming**. Abhay has written several articles to promote computer programming, and has conducted teacher-training workshops to encourage aspiring teachers to experiment with this idea.

Abhay has been associated with the Software Industry since 1988 as a programmer, engineer, entrepreneur, and a trainer. After getting an MS in Computer Engineering from Syracuse University (USA), he worked as a programmer for product companies that developed operating systems, network protocols, and secure software. In 1997, Abhay co-founded Disha Technologies, a successful software services organization.

Programming remains one of Abhay's favorite hobbies, and he continues to explore the "entertaining, intellectual, and educational" aspects of programming.

Table of Contents

My basic idea is that programming is the most powerful medium of developing the sophisticated and rigorous thinking needed for mathematics, for grammar, for physics, for statistics, for all the "hard" subjects.... In short, I believe more than ever that programming should be a key part of the intellectual development of people growing up.

- Seymour Papert

Design Process

This book is organized as a series of independent Scratch projects – each of which describes how to design and build an interesting and challenging Scratch program. Every project follows a certain common design methodology. The purpose of this chapter is to get you familiarized with this methodology, so that you will then be able to explore any project without difficulty.

Divide and conquer technique

We build each program *incrementally*, i.e. we use a methodology called "Divide and Conquer". Let us see an example to understand how to go about using this technique.

In the "divide and conquer" approach, we take a step back and take a careful look at our final program and ask the question, "*What is this program made up of? Can we break it up into separate parts that are meaningful and possibly reusable?*"

Once we identify such components of the program, we go about designing each of them separately.

In other words, we call our complete program as the "Big Idea" and break it down into smaller *feature ideas*. We list these various feature ideas in what is called the "high level design".

For example, if we wanted to design the house shown below, we would first take a step back and take a keen look at the house and ask the question: "What is this house made up of? Can we break it apart into meaningful reusable components or parts?"

We come up with the answer: "Yes, we see three parts: a wall, a roof, and a window."

  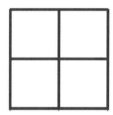

Then, it is a matter of designing each of these components (*wall* which is a square, *roof* which is a sitting triangle, and *window* which is a 2x2 pattern of squares) separately and putting them together to get a house.

There are several advantages of using this "divide and conquer" methodology, some of which are listed below:

1. It simplifies our overall task considerably. In the *house* program, designing a square, a triangle, etc. is simpler than designing the entire house at once. It is also much easier to go back and correct problems or mistakes in these smaller components.
2. The components can be reused. In the *house* program, the square design used for the wall can be reused in the window design.
3. The final program becomes much more flexible. In the *house* program, by drawing walls, roofs, and windows of different sizes we can draw houses of different kind and size.

How do we identify the smaller feature ideas in our Scratch programs? We do that first by playing with the actual running program (whose Internet link I have provided at the beginning of every chapter). Then we take a keen look at the main screen of the program and try to identify its different pieces, such as, sprites, the function of each of them, and how they interact.

We list these feature ideas in a section called the "High Level Design".

Incremental design

The next step is to actually design these various feature ideas one by one. This design process is generally stated as below:

1. Take a smaller feature idea (a part of the "big idea").
2. Think about how it can be implemented (experiment in Scratch if necessary).
3. Write the scripts.
4. Test and verify that the scripts work as expected. If not, repeat steps 2, 3, and 4 until the idea works as expected.
5. Repeat from step 1 (take up another smaller feature idea). Continue until all required features have been added to the program.

Flow of Each Chapter

As already mentioned, the book consists of a series of independent Scratch projects. Every chapter follows a certain common flow and structure. I will now get you familiarized with this structure, so that you will then be able to pick any project and go through its flow with ease.

All project chapters contain the same sections as listed (and explained) below.

Program Description

In this section we describe how the final program is used by its users. If it's a game, we will describe the rules of the game; if it's an interactive animation we will describe what the animation does, and so on.

I will then provide an Internet link (URL) to a working Scratch version of the program which you should check out. I encourage you to explore the program and its various features before reading the chapter further. But, be sure not to look at the Scratch scripts of the program, because we want to design them ourselves.

How to run the program:

This section will describe the steps to run the program. For example, typically the first step of most Scratch programs is to click the Green flag.

As shown below, I provide a screenshot of the program and the URL. You can click either on the image itself or on the URL to open the project in your browser.

<Internet URL to the actual program>

Scratch and CS Concepts Used

This section lists the Scratch and CS concepts that you will need to know when you design this program. I assume that you are already familiar with these concepts. If not, or if you want to brush up on these concepts, you should refer to the freely downloadable supplement to this book at http://www.abhayjoshi.net/scratch/book1/supplement.pdf.

Main concepts:

This section gives a list of all Scratch and CS concepts used in the main program.

Additional concepts (used in the advanced version):

Some programs include an "advanced version" – which contains a few optional advanced features. This section lists the additional concepts – if any – that you need to know to design these advanced features.

High Level Design

This is where we list the multiple smaller ideas which can be programmed separately. We have already discussed the "divide and conquer" technique above. We study the main screen of the program (as shown below) and try to come up with this list of feature ideas.

<Screenshot of the main screen of the program>

Program Versions

A "program version" is nothing but a copy of your Scratch project with a unique name. In the process of designing our Scratch program step by step, we will develop multiple program versions, such as, project-1, project-2, etc. Each version will include a subset of the feature ideas. As the version number increases, it indicates that the program has more and more features.

Initial Version

We begin with a collection of a few basic feature ideas and implement them as the first version of the program.

As shown below I will go through each feature idea. For each idea, I will describe it briefly, discuss a possible "design" that will allow us to program this idea, and finally present a "solution" that presents details of Scratch scripts. For each feature idea, you should try to think of your own design and solution before reading the ones that I propose.

Solutions to all feature ideas are provided in the last section.

Feature Idea # 1

<Idea description>

Design:

<Step-by-step description of how this idea can be designed.>

Feature Idea # 2

Same steps as idea #1, and so on.

Save as Program Version 1

Before continuing to the next set of ideas, you make a copy of the project under a different name. (For example, I am calling my copy as Dummy-1). This way, you have a backup of your project that you can go back to if required for any reason.

Next Set of Features/ideas

Here, we list the next set of feature ideas that we will design and program in the next version of the project.

And so on

This process of listing ideas, implementing each of them separately, and creating a project version continues until we finish all the planned features.

Solutions to Feature Ideas

In this section, the solutions to all features ideas for this project are presented. You should look at these solutions only after trying every idea yourself.

That's all! You are now ready to jump to any of the projects presented in this book. Good luck!

Project 1: Game of Bricks

Game Description

This is a game you play with a ball and a flat paddle. A number of bricks are lined up at the top of the screen. As the ball bounces up and down you use the paddle to hit the bricks and score points. The ball must not touch the ground: after 3 such touches you lose the game. If you hit all the bricks you win the game. You can control the difficulty level of the game by changing the speed of the ball.

Do you want to check out a working Scratch version of this program? Click on the image below (or the URL just below it). I encourage you to explore the program and its various features. But, don't look at the Scratch scripts yet; we want to design this program ourselves!

How to play the game:
1. Click on the "Green flag": everything is reset to the original state.
2. Set ball speed using the slider.
3. Press SPACE BAR to start the game.

Link: https://scratch.mit.edu/projects/104716301/

Scratch and CS Concepts Used

When we design this program, we will make use of the following Scratch and CS concepts. I assume that you are already familiar with these concepts. If not, or if you want to brush up on these concepts, you should refer to the free downloadable supplement to this book at http://www.abhayjoshi.net/scratch/book1/supplement.pdf.

Main concepts:

- Algorithms
- Backdrops - multiple
- Concurrency - running scripts in parallel
- Concurrency - race condition
- Conditionals (IF)
- Conditionals (Wait until)
- Costumes
- Events
- Looping - simple (repeat, forever)
- Motion - absolute
- Motion - relative
- Motion - smooth using repeat
- Relational operators (=, <, >)
- Sensing
- Sequence
- Stopping scripts
- Synchronization using broadcasting
- User events (keyboard)
- User events (mouse)
- Variables - numbers
- Variables - as remote control
- Variables - properties (built-in)
- XY Geometry

Additional concepts (for the advanced version):

- OOP - creating instances using clones
- Random numbers

High Level Design:

Let's take a look at the main screen of the game and point out the different pieces.

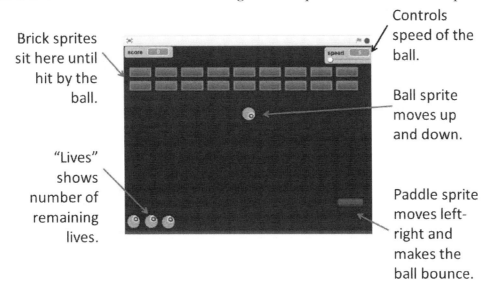

Brick sprites sit here until hit by the ball.

Controls speed of the ball.

Ball sprite moves up and down.

"Lives" shows number of remaining lives.

Paddle sprite moves left-right and makes the ball bounce.

The order in which we should work on these different pieces of the program is really up to us. It probably makes sense to first get the ball bouncing around the screen. Then, we will add a paddle that can be moved by the user. The ball must bounce off the paddle. Next, we will add the bricks which must disappear upon touching the ball. Next, we will add the idea of "number of lives" to the game. Finally, there are a few little things that will wrap up the game, such as variables to count things, controlling the speed of the ball, etc.

So, let's get rolling with these various ideas one by one. Be sure to try writing your own scripts for each idea before looking up the "Solutions" section.

Initial Version

In the initial version of the program, we will work on the following feature ideas:

-   Get a "ball" sprite and make it bounce freely. After pressing SPACE BAR the ball should start bouncing around, primarily in the vertical direction.
-   Add the paddle. The paddle should move left-right only and follow the mouse pointer. The ball should bounce off the paddle.

For this initial version, give your project a special name (using "Save as"). For example, I am calling my copy as Bricks-1.

Feature Idea # 1: Bouncing ball

Get a "ball" sprite and make it bounce freely. After pressing SPACE BAR the ball should start bouncing around in the vertical direction.

Design:

I think this is so easy you can straightaway write the script. You already know how to get free motion in the horizontal direction. So, the only tricky challenge is to make the ball move up and down.

Hint: Think about setting the ball's direction before it starts moving.

Feature Idea # 2: Paddle

Add the paddle. This involves two steps.

Step 1: The paddle should move left-right only and follow the mouse pointer.

Design:

How will you ensure that the paddle only moves horizontally?

Well, we can do that by keeping its Y coordinate fixed. So, whatever commands we use the paddle's Y coordinate must not change.

And, how will you make the paddle follow the mouse pointer?

Since Y is not to change, the paddle's X coordinate will *continuously* vary according to the pointer's X coordinate. In other words, the paddle's X coordinate will always be *equal* to the pointer's X coordinate.

Hint: The "set x" command sets the sprite's X coordinate, and the "mouse x" property (under "Sensing") gives the pointer's X coordinate.

Step 2: Make the ball bounce off the paddle.

Design:

First, you will need to teach the ball to sense when it touches the paddle.

You can use the "touching" condition in an IF statement.

"Bouncing" actually is a complex idea (think about reflection of light), but for now we will keep it simple: we will assume that bouncing essentially means turning around and moving away. The turning angle must be large. You can experiment and try different values.

Save Program Version 1

Before continuing to the next set of ideas, we will save our project. This way, we have a backup of our project that we can go back to if required for any reason.

Compare your program with my program at the link below.

Bricks-1: includes ideas 1 and 2 explained above.
Link: https://scratch.mit.edu/projects/104538051/

How to play the game:
1. Click on the "Green flag": everything is reset to the original state.
2. Press SPACE BAR to start.
3. The ball starts bouncing up and down, and you can move the paddle left-right by moving the mouse pointer.

Next Set of Features/ideas:
1. Add bricks and make them work as expected. We will do this in three steps.
    a. Insert one brick sprite. The brick should appear at the start of the game and disappear when the ball touches it. Add a "score" variable, which will increase by 1 when the brick is hit by the ball.
    b. Next, duplicate the brick sprite to have multiple bricks. The script for each will be identical.
    c. Stop the game when all bricks have been hit, and declare victory.
2. Add a "speed" slider variable to control the speed of the ball.

For this version, make a copy of your project (using "Save as") under a different name. For example, I am calling my copy as Bricks-2.

Feature Idea # 3: Bricks
Add bricks and make them work as expected.

Note that we can design just one brick sprite and then duplicate it to have as many as desired – I have 18 in my program. We will do this in three steps.

<u>Step 1</u>: *Insert one brick sprite. The brick should appear at the start of the game and disappear when the ball touches it. Keep "score", which will increase by 1 when the brick is hit by the ball.*

Design:
Sensing that the ball has touched the brick is straightforward: it would be similar to the

way we did the paddle and ball above.

Score will be maintained by a variable called "score". The brick needs to follow the following algorithm after the game starts:

```
Show
Wait (Do nothing) until it touches the ball
Bump up the "score" variable by 1
Hide
```

Step 2: _Next, duplicate the brick sprite to have multiple bricks. The script for each will be identical._

This is self-explanatory! Just make sure the bricks are laid out nicely in rows.

Step 3: _Stop the game when all bricks have been hit, and declare victory._

Design:

We now have the "score" variable to count the number of hits. When it equals the number of bricks, we will know that the game has been won. The stage can do this work using an additional script. Its algorithm will be as follows:

```
Wait until the score is 18
Declare "win"
Stop the game
```

Feature Idea # 4: Control speed
Allow the user to set the speed of the ball.

Design:
How will you arrange things so that the user can set the speed of the ball?

The speed of the ball is decided by the "move" command. Bigger the input of "move", higher the speed would be. So, you could use a variable in place of move's input. By displaying this variable as a "slider" you can allow the user to control its value.

Save as Program Version 2
Before continuing to the next set of ideas, we will save our project. This way, we will have another backup of our project that we can go back to if required for any reason.

Compare your program with my program at the link below.

Bricks-2: includes ideas 3 and 4 explained above.

Link: https://scratch.mit.edu/projects/104712575/

How to play the game:

1. Click on the "Green flag": everything is reset to the original state.
2. Set ball speed using the slider.
3. Press SPACE BAR to start the game.

Final Set of Features/ideas:

1. Implement the "number of lives" feature. We should see the number of lives as a set of balls. Every time the ball touches the ground (lower edge of the screen), we should see one ball less. When all lives are used, the program should declare that we lost.
2. Right now the ball doesn't bounce off the bricks; it just goes through them. Make it bounce off the bricks.

For this final version, make a copy of your project (using "Save as") under a different name. For example, I am calling my copy as Bricks-final.

Feature Idea # 5: Number of lives

Implement the "number of lives" feature. We should see the number of lives as number of balls. Every time the ball touches the ground (lower edge of the screen), we should see one ball less. When all lives are used, the program should declare that we lost.

We will do this in 3 steps. In step 1, we will use a variable to count the number of lives. In step 2, we will actually show the number of lives (as balls) on the screen. And in step 3, we will ensure the game declares "You lose!" when all lives have been used.

Step 1: Add a variable called "lives" which will track the number of "lives". Every time the ball touches the ground, one life is lost. If the game allows, say 3 lives, the game should stop after 3 touches.

Design:

How will you make the ball sense that it has touched the bottom edge of the screen?

Well, there is no special command "if touching bottom edge", so we will have to improvise. We will color the bottom edge of the stage to represent "ground", and then use the "touching color" condition in an IF statement. After every touch, we will decrement the *lives* variable. And, when *lives* becomes 0, we will stop the game.

Design:

We will do this by using a new sprite called "lives". This sprite will have 3 costumes – showing 3, 2, and 1 ball(s) respectively. By tracking the "lives" variable, this sprite can show the appropriate costume. Its algorithm will be as below:

```
Show the 3 ball costume
Wait until lives = 2
Show the 2 ball costume
Wait until lives = 1
Show the 1 ball costume
Wait until lives = 0
Hide
```

Draw the sprite (along with its 3 costumes) and write a script for the above algorithm.

Step 3: *Add another screen to declare when the game is lost.*

Design:

The stage will have a new backdrop to declare "loss". The ball sprite knows when the game is lost with the help of the following script:

We can send a broadcast to the stage from this script. After receiving the message the stage will switch to the "loss" backdrop.

Feature Idea # 6: Bounce off the bricks

Make the ball bounce off the bricks also.

Design:

When the ball touches a brick, two things need to happen: (1) the ball should bounce off the brick, and (2) the brick should disappear. We have already done the second part by having the brick "sense" the touch. To do the first part, the ball will need to sense the touch as well.

If we ask both the ball and the brick to do the sensing, we risk having a "race condition" – a condition in which two entities are actively checking for a single event and one of them is likely to miss it. (See Concepts appendix for a detailed explanation of "race condition").

To avoid this race condition, only one of the touching parties (ball or brick) should sense the touch and inform the other via broadcast.

Save as Program Version "Final"

Congratulations! You have completed all the main features of the game. As before, let's save this project before continuing to the advanced ideas. Compare your program with my program at the link below.

Bricks-final: includes ideas 5 and 6 explained above.

Link: https://scratch.mit.edu/projects/104716301/

How to play the game:
1. Click on the "Green flag": everything is reset to the original state.
2. Set ball speed using the slider.
3. Press SPACE BAR to start the game.

Advanced Features

We can make several improvements in our program as listed below. These features are optional, so, implement only those that you find interesting and useful.

For this advanced version, make a copy of your project (using "Save as") under a different name. For example, I am calling my copy as Bricks-adv.

Feature Idea # 7: Correct bouncing

We have implemented the action of "bouncing" off the paddle (and bricks) quite arbitrarily. Make it more realistic (like the Scratch command "if on edge bounce").

Design:

Presently, our program just uses a "turn 150" command to implement bouncing off the paddle. The angle 150 is quite arbitrary. That is not how real-life bouncing works. The Scratch command "If on edge bounce" is a great example of realistic bouncing. So, let's understand how that command works.

In Scratch, the "direction" property of a sprite indicates its angle with North. So, 0 means North, 90 means East, -90 means West, and so on.

When a sprite bounces off a vertical edge (left or right), its "direction" changes only in sign. So, 30 becomes -30, -110 becomes 110, and so on. When the sprite bounces off a horizontal edge (top or bottom), its "direction" after the bounce is 180-A where A is its direction before the bounce.

That is how the "If on edge bounce" command calculates the turning angle.

To keep things simple, we will only consider vertical bouncing for both the paddle and the bricks.

Modify your bouncing scripts and then compare with the solution given in the "Solutions" section.

Feature Idea # 8: Layout of the bricks

Laying out the bricks manually is tedious and may not give a perfectly uniform look. Make this task of brick placement programmatic (i.e. through your scripts) and remove the manual error.

Design:

The idea basically is to find a way to calculate the x and y coordinates of each brick and use the "Go To" command. We will use variables to do this.

Let's say, variables *firstX* and *firstY* show the location of the top-left brick, and variables "L" and "H" show the length and height of each brick (plus some empty space). Using these variables, we can lay out the bricks neatly in two rows.

The following table shows a few examples of how these variables can be used to calculate positions of bricks:

Brick	X coordinate	Y coordinate
1st brick in first row	firstX	firstY
5th brick in first row	firstX + (4*L)	firstY
3rd brick in second row	firstX + (2*L)	firstY – (1*H)
3rd brick in fourth row	firstX + (2*L)	firstY – (3*H)

In general, we can deduce the following equations to give the x and y coordinates of any brick:

x = firstX + (column # – 1) * L

y = firstY – (row # – 1) * H

For example, the following script will position a brick in the 4ᵗʰ place in the 1ˢᵗ row:

Someone in our Scratch program will need to set these four variables to appropriate values at the very beginning (when green flag is clicked). The stage would be a good candidate for that work. More importantly, the bricks must position themselves *after* the variables have been set. We can ensure this by using *broadcasting*. The stage will send a broadcast message after the variables have been set, and each brick will act upon receiving this message.

For example, the script below is for the 3ʳᵈ brick in the 2ⁿᵈ row:

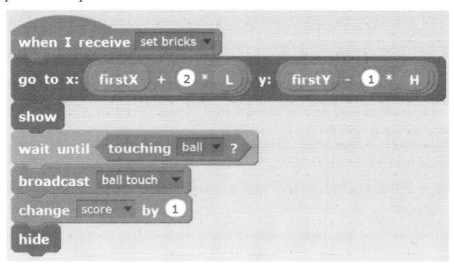

Feature Idea # 9: Clones for bricks

You might have seen that it is tedious to use multiple sprites for bricks since any change requires a lot of duplication of work. If we use the idea of "clones", we just need one brick sprite.

Design:

The main (parent) brick will itself remain hidden, but create the required number of clones. It will also set x and y variables which each clone can use to position itself correctly.

Algorithm:

For the parent brick:

```
Hide
Set y            // first row
Repeat 2         // for each row
   Set x         // first brick
   Repeat 9      // for each brick in this row
      Create clone
      Change x   // next brick
   End repeat
   Change y      // second row
End repeat
```

And then, each clone will run the following algorithm:

```
Go to x, y
Wait until touches ball
Send message to ball
Increment "score"
Delete clone
```

Save as Program Version "Advanced"

Congratulations! You have completed all the advanced features of the game. As before, let's save this project.

Compare your program with my program at the link below.

Bricks-adv: includes the advanced features listed above.

Link: https://scratch.mit.edu/projects/104716140/

How to play the game:
1. Click on the "Green flag": everything is reset to original state.
2. Set ball speed using the slider.
3. Press SPACE BAR to start the game.

Additional Challenge(s)

Sometimes the ball starts moving perfectly horizontally. When that happens, there is no alternative but to restart the game. Can you add a script to detect this condition and alter the ball's movement?

Design:

We can use the "direction" property of the ball sprite to detect this condition. Fixing it is easy: just nudge the ball in a different direction by turning.

Solutions to Feature Ideas

Feature Idea # 1:

Script for the "Ball" sprite:

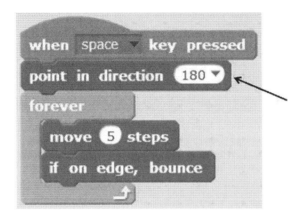

To ensure the ball starts its motion up and down.

Feature Idea # 2:

Step 1:

Script for the "paddle" sprite:

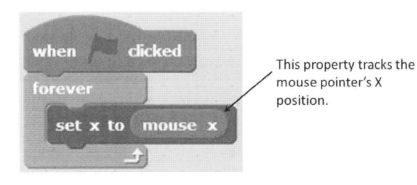

This property tracks the mouse pointer's X position.

Step 2:

Script for the "ball" sprite:

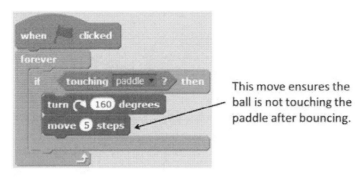

This move ensures the ball is not touching the paddle after bouncing.

Feature Idea # 3:

Step 1:
Script for the "brick" sprite:

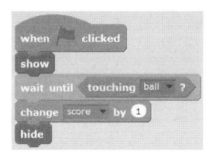

Note that someone will need to initialize the "score" variable to 0 at the start of the game. You can really have any sprite do this. But, since this variable isn't tied (or related) to any particular sprite, it's a good policy to let the Stage do this initialization.

Step 3:
Script for the "stage":

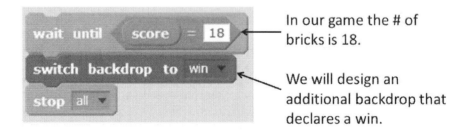

In our game the # of bricks is 18.

We will design an additional backdrop that declares a win.

Feature Idea # 4:
The "speed" variable as a slider:

Script for the "ball" sprite:

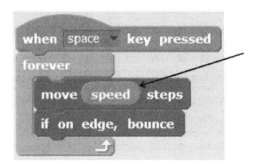

As the value of "speed" changes the actual speed of the sprite will also change.

Feature Idea # 5:

<u>Step 1</u>:
Script for the "ball" sprite:

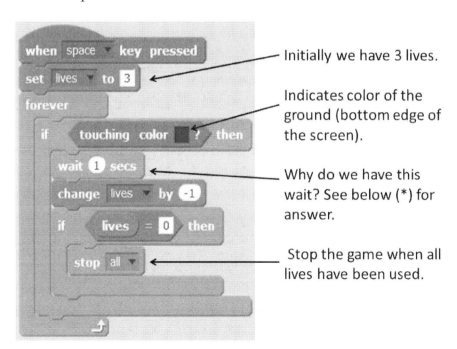

Initially we have 3 lives.

Indicates color of the ground (bottom edge of the screen).

Why do we have this wait? See below (*) for answer.

Stop the game when all lives have been used.

* Without this wait statement, it is possible that the forever loop would sense a single touch multiple times and decrement the variable more than once. See it for yourself.

With this "wait" added the other motion script would have taken the ball away preventing multiple decrements.

Step 2:
Script for the "lives" sprite:

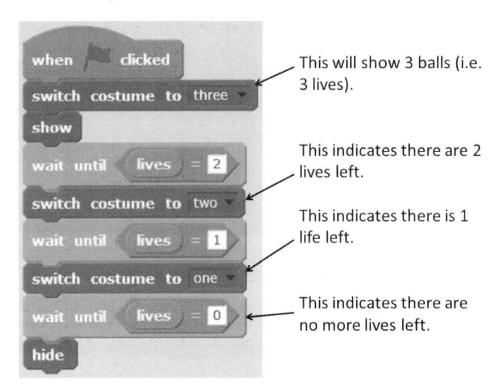

This will show 3 balls (i.e. 3 lives).

This indicates there are 2 lives left.

This indicates there is 1 life left.

This indicates there are no more lives left.

Step 3:

We can insert a broadcast in this script as shown below:

The stage will receive the broadcast and use a new backdrop called "lose":

Feature Idea # 6:

Every brick sprite will send a broadcast after touching the ball:

The ball sprite will receive the broadcast and bounce:

Feature Idea # 7:

Script for the "ball" sprite:

We will add a slight randomness to ensure the ball doesn't get stuck in some fixed pattern.

Feature Idea # 8:

Solution is discussed in the design section itself.

Feature Idea # 9:

Refer to the program file for the advanced version.

Additional challenge:

Script for the "ball" sprite:

Computer programming is an art form, in an aesthetic sense. When we prepare a program, the experience can be just like composing poetry or music...Some programs are elegant, some are exquisite, some are sparkling. ... Computer programming is an art, because it applies accumulated knowledge to the world, because it requires skill and ingenuity, and especially because it produces objects of beauty. – Donald Knuth

Project 2: Square Designs

Program Description

This is a program that draws a few interesting "square" designs. A number of buttons (with names of designs as labels) are lined up at the bottom of the screen. When you click one of them, a design is drawn on the screen. You can control the resulting design by entering some inputs, such as, the size of each square.

Do you want to check out a working Scratch version of this program? Click on the image below (or the URL just below it). I encourage you to explore the program and its various features. But, don't look at the Scratch scripts yet; we want to design this program ourselves!

How to run the program:

1. Click on the "Green flag": everything is reset to original state.
2. Select a design by clicking one of the buttons.
3. Enter inputs if prompted and watch the design.

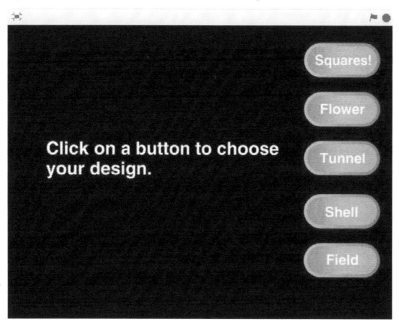

Link: https://scratch.mit.edu/projects/104974438/

Scratch and CS Concepts Used

When we design this program, we will make use of the following Scratch and CS concepts. I assume that you are already familiar with these concepts. If not, or if you want to brush up on these concepts, you should refer to the free downloadable supplement to this book at http://www.abhayjoshi.net/scratch/book1/supplement.pdf.

Main concepts:

- Arithmetic operators (+, -, *, /)
- Arithmetic expressions
- Backdrops - multiple
- Events
- Procedures with inputs
- Geometry - square, circle, triangle, spiral
- Looping - simple (repeat, forever)
- Looping - nested
- Looping - conditional (repeat until)
- Motion - absolute
- Motion - relative
- Pen commands
- Random numbers
- Relational operators (=, <, >)
- Sequence
- Synchronization using broadcasting
- User events (mouse)
- User input (ASK)
- User input (buttons)
- XY Geometry

Additional concepts (for the advanced version):

- Logic operators (and, or, not)

High Level Design:

This is where we take a step back from the computer (literally!), analyze the problem in our mind (and on a piece of paper if necessary), and break it down into multiple smaller ideas which can be programmed separately.

Let's take a look at the various drawings created by the program and try to point out the different pieces. The program draws the following 4 types of designs:

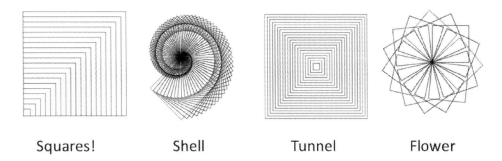

Squares!   Shell   Tunnel   Flower

The order in which we should work on these different square designs is really up to us. We will have one sprite (maybe the "pencil" sprite) do all the drawing. The buttons will just send messages to the pencil sprite which will then draw the appropriate design.

Does that sound like a good strategy?

You will notice that the basic shape used in all the drawings is a *square*. So, it would be natural to begin with a script that draws a square. We can then convert this script into a procedure (a new block) called "square". This procedure should take a "size" input to be able to draw squares of any size.

Next, we will consider separately each of the four designs (Squares!, Flower, Shell, and Tunnel) and figure out how to draw it.

So, let's get rolling with these various ideas one by one. Be sure to try writing your own scripts for each idea before looking up the "Solutions" section.

Initial Version
1. Write a new procedure (a new Scratch command block) that can draw a square of any size.
2. Write a script that will draw the "Squares!" design.

For this initial version, give your project a special name (using "Save as"). For example, I am calling my copy as Squares-1.

Feature Idea # 1: The Square procedure
Write a new procedure (a new Scratch command block) that can draw a square of any size.

Design:
To draw a square, we need to draw a straight line and take a right (or left) turn, and

repeat these steps four times. Write a script that will draw a square of length 100. Next, convert this script to a new procedure called "Square". Finally, add an input called *length* that will determine the size of the square.

Feature Idea # 2: The Squares! design

Write a script that will draw the "Squares!" design.

Design:

Let's take a look at the design itself:

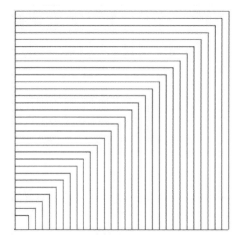

How will you draw this design using our *Square* procedure?

Here is an idea: If your drawing sprite positions itself at the lower left corner, points up, and draws square after square – increasing size slightly for each, you will get this design! Let's test this approach by a simple script as shown below:

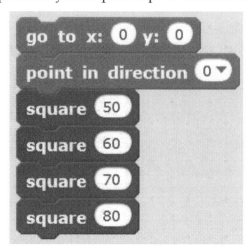

Our hunch is correct! We get 4 squares in the required pattern as shown below.

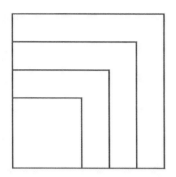

It would obviously be very tedious to draw a large number of squares (say 20) using the above approach of having a long list of "square" commands. It would be nice to use "repeat". But, to be able to use "repeat" we must have an identical set of commands. Can you think of a way to make the square commands above *appear* identical?

Well, we can use the idea of variables. If we have a variable called *size* for the length of the square, we can convert the above code as below:

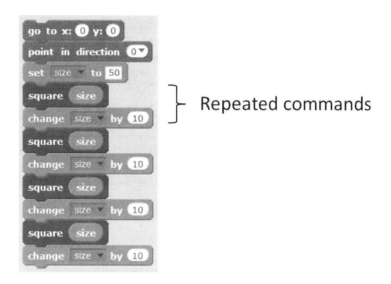

} Repeated commands

Now, we have a repeatable set of commands. You can write the final script.

Save as Program Version 1

Before continuing to the next set of ideas, we will save our project. This way, we have a backup of our project that we can go back to if required for any reason.

Compare your program with my program at the link below.

Squares-1: includes ideas 1 and 2 explained above.
Link: https://scratch.mit.edu/projects/104973260/

How to run the program:
1. Click on the "Green flag": everything is reset to the original state.
2. Press "S" to draw the squares design.

Next Set of Features/ideas:
1. Write a script that will draw the "flower" design.
2. Write a script that will draw the "tunnel" design.

For this version, make a copy of your project (using "Save as") under a different name. For example, I am calling my copy as Squares-2.

Feature Idea # 3: The Flower design
Write a script that will draw the "flower" design.

Design:
Let's take a look at the design itself. We will try a few different inputs:

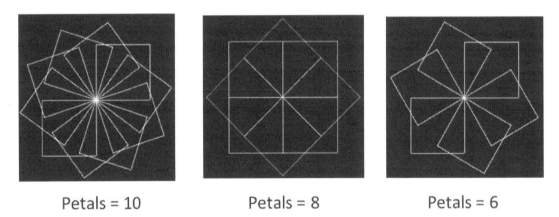

| Petals = 10 | Petals = 8 | Petals = 6 |

Can you figure out how these designs are drawn?

It appears that the square shape has been drawn multiple times while keeping it fixed at one of its corners. It's as if we pinned a square-shaped paper cut-out at its lower left corner, drew its outline, turned the cut-out by a small angle, and repeated this process a number of times. Let's test this hypothesis.

We already have our "square" procedure. We also know that turning the paper cut-out is the same as changing the orientation of the pencil sprite (which does the drawing). Let's see what the following instructions do:

```
go to x: 0 y: 0
point in direction 0▼
square 100
turn ↻ 20 degrees
square 100
turn ↻ 20 degrees
square 100
turn ↻ 20 degrees
square 100
turn ↻ 20 degrees
square 100
turn ↻ 20 degrees
```

We get this design:

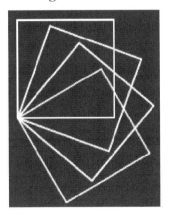

So, our hunch is correct!

It's also obvious that we can employ the use of "repeat" as shown below.

```
go to x: 0 y: 0
point in direction 0▼
repeat 4
    square 100
    turn ↻ 20 degrees
```

Now, how do we draw a complete flower of squares such that it looks symmetric and complete? Clearly, we will have to increase the *count* input of REPEAT. What should this count be to create a symmetric and complete flower?

Well, we can apply our knowledge of school geometry to our advantage. We know that the total angle the sprite turns through in one complete spin around itself is 360. So, obviously, all we have to do to get a nice-looking complete flower is to ensure that the sum of all turns is 360.

Feature Idea # 4: The Tunnel design

Write a script that will draw the "tunnel" design.

Design:

Let us take a look at the drawing itself and try to understand how it is drawn:

It appears that the design consists of several squares all having the same center. In other words, they are "concentric". To understand how to make this design, let us run the program again to draw fewer squares (as shown below).

Our "square" procedure draws squares starting from the lower-left corner. If we draw the smallest square first, the sprite would have to jump to another point before drawing the next square.

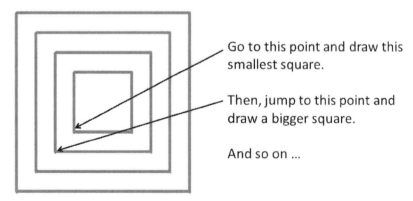

Go to this point and draw this smallest square.

Then, jump to this point and draw a bigger square.

And so on ...

The question is how do we compute the x and y of this next point?

See the figure below:

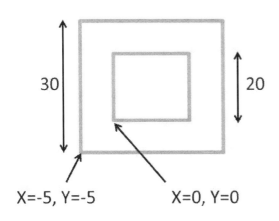

Let's say the first square of size 20 is drawn starting at x=0, y=0. The next square is of size 30 (that is, larger by 10). For this square to have the same center as the first one, its starting point will have to be x=-5, y=-5.

In other words, both x and y will have to change by *half* of the difference in lengths (which is 10).

Let's test this hypothesis:

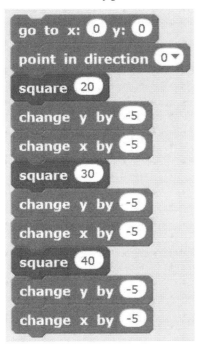

With this script, we get:

So, our basic premise is correct.

It would obviously be very tedious to draw a large number of squares (say 20) using this approach. It would be nice to use "repeat". But, to be able to use "repeat" we must have an identical set of commands. How will you convert the above list of commands (square, change y, change x) such that each trio *appears* identical?

Well, once again, we can use the idea of variables. If we have a variable called *size* for the length of the square, we can convert the above code as below:

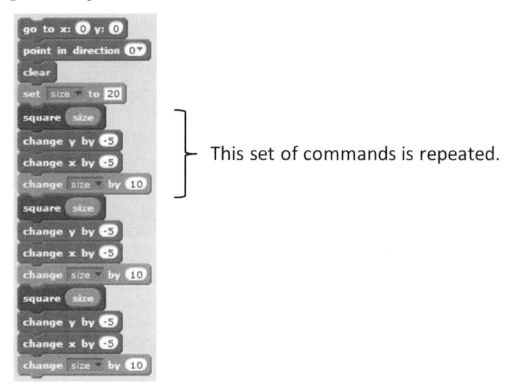

This set of commands is repeated.

We get the same design! And, we also have a repeatable set of commands.

Save as Program Version 2

Before continuing to the next set of ideas, we will save our project. This way, we have a backup of our project that we can go back to if required for any reason.

Compare your program with my program at the link below.

Squares-2: includes ideas 3 and 4 explained above.
Link: https://scratch.mit.edu/projects/104974061/

How to run the program:

1. Click on the "Green flag": everything is reset to the original state.
2. Press "s" to draw the squares design, and "t" to draw the tunnel design.

Final Set of Features/ideas:

1. Write a script that will draw the "shell" design.
2. Create buttons to draw each of the designs.
3. Right now, all designs only draw a fixed number of squares. Allow the user to decide how many squares each design should have.
4. Right now, the buttons remain visible and block the screen partially. Hide them when drawing is in progress.

For this final version, make a copy of your project (using "Save as") under a different name. For example, I am calling my copy as Squares-final.

Feature Idea # 5: The Shell design

Write a script that will draw the "shell" design.

Design:

Let's take a look at the design itself:

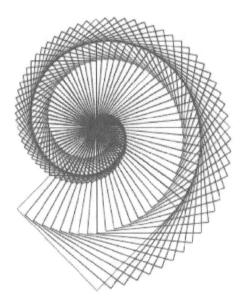

At first look, this design appears to have no relation with squares. But it does! Look carefully.

This design follows an approach similar to the "flower" design. The square shape has been drawn multiple times while keeping it fixed at its lower-left corner. The difference (from the "flower" design) is that the size of the square is increased a little every time. Let's test this hypothesis.

Since we need a large number of squares, it is better if we employ the use of "repeat". We will use the "size" variable to ensure the square increases in size gradually.

With this script, we get:

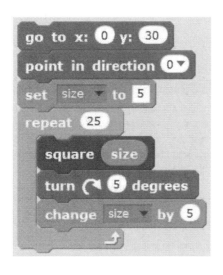

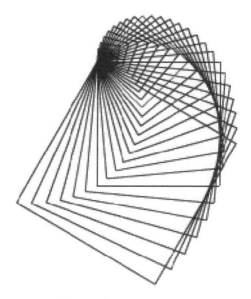

So, our hunch is correct! To get the final design, we will need to experiment with the different numbers. After some trial and error, you can write the final script.

Feature Idea # 6: Buttons

Provide buttons for each of the designs.

Design and Solution:

We can do this easily by using broadcasting. When a button is clicked, it will send a unique broadcast message. The drawing sprite (pencil) will receive it and draw the respective design.

For example, the following script is for the "flower" button:

And this is the "receiving" script for the drawing sprite (pencil):

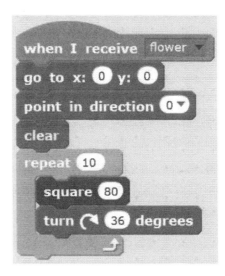

We can have similar broadcasting connections for the other buttons.

Feature Idea # 7: User control

Right now, all designs only draw a fixed number of squares. Allow the user to decide how many squares each design should have.

The Squares! Design:

As it is, this design draws 20 squares. Making it flexible is straightforward – we just have to use the "ask" command to ask the user for the number of squares, and use the "answer" variable as input to "repeat".

Write this script yourself and then compare it with the one given below.

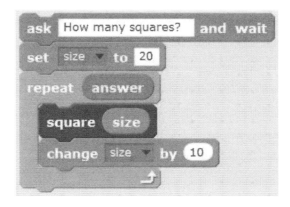

The Flower Design:

Right now, this design uses 10 petals. To draw flowers of any number of petals, we can once again ask the user through the "Ask" command. Remember that the "turn" command turns by 36 degrees to ensure that the total of all turns is 360 degrees (10 x 36). We will need to take care that the turning angle remains such that the total is always 360 degrees.

Write this script yourself and then compare it with the one given below.

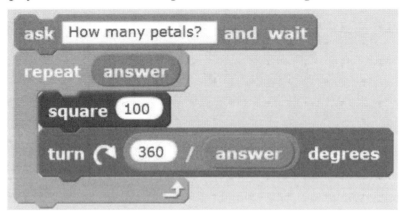

The Tunnel Design:

Right now, the design contains 20 squares. Making this flexible is very simple. Just ask the user once again and use the "answer" variable as input to "repeat".

Write this script yourself and then compare it with the one given here.

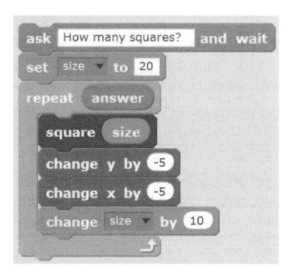

Feature Idea # 8: Clean screen

Right now, the buttons remain visible and block the screen partially. It would be nice to hide them when drawing is in progress.

Design:

This idea is very easy to implement using "broadcasting". Every time a button is clicked it will send a message asking all buttons to hide. The buttons will show up again when you click the green flag.

Save as Program Version "Final"

Congratulations! You have completed all the main features of the program. As before, let's save this project before continuing to the advanced ideas.

Compare your program with my program at the link below.

Squares-final: includes ideas 5 thru 8 explained above.
Link: https://scratch.mit.edu/projects/104974438/

How to run the program:

1. Click on the "Green flag": everything is reset to the original state.
2. Select a design by clicking one of the buttons.
3. Enter inputs if prompted and watch the design.

Design Steps – Advanced Version

We will include the "Field" design in the advanced version. Plus, we can make several improvements in the basic version as listed below. These features are optional, so, implement only those that you find interesting and useful.

For this advanced version, make a copy of your project (using "Save as") under a different name. For example, I am calling my copy as Squares-adv.

Feature Idea # 9: Fit the Squares! design

One problem with the "Squares!" design is that it cannot fit more than 30 squares. The design goes out of range (the visible screen) and becomes distorted. Fix the design such that any number of squares will fit on the visible screen.

Design:

This is an interesting challenge.

First, let's understand the problem. We know that the height of the Scratch screen is

360 (Y varies from -180 at the bottom to 180 at the top). To keep some margin from both ends, we start drawing at y = -150 and stop when the top end of the design is y = 150. That means we have 300 pixels available before the design goes out of range. Since the gap between each pair of squares is 10, we can fit 300/10 = 30 squares.

What if we wanted to fit more squares in this same range, say, 50 or 100? We would obviously have to reduce the *gap* between squares. In order to fit *any* number of squares within the available range of 300 pixels, we could use the following formula:

```
Number of squares = 300 / Gap
```

So,

```
Gap = 300 / Number of squares
```

And that is our solution! We just have to modify our script to use this formula for the gap. We will create another variable called *gap* for the gap between squares.

Feature Idea # 10: Fit the Tunnel design

One problem with the "Tunnel" design is that it cannot fit more than 30 squares. The design goes out of range (the visible screen) and becomes distorted. Fix the design such that any number of squares will fit on the visible screen.

Design:

This challenge is similar to the one we addressed in the idea above.

First, let's understand the problem. Once again, the constraint is the height of the Scratch screen which is 360. Since each square of the tunnel is 10 pixels bigger than the previous square, it is obvious that we can fit 300/10 = 30 squares.

Note that the actual gap between each pair of squares is 5 (which is *half* of the change in size).

In order to fit *any* number of squares within the available range of 300 pixels, we obviously have to calculate the *gap* between squares. We can use the following formula:

```
Gap = (300 / Number of squares) / 2
```

And that is our solution! We just have to modify our script to use this formula for the gap.

Feature Idea # 11: Fit the Flower design

One problem with the "Flower" design is that it cannot fit squares bigger than 120. The design goes out of range (the visible screen) and becomes distorted. Fix the design such that this doesn't happen.

Design:

Unlike the "tunnel" or "squares!" designs, the problem with the "flower" design is not the *number of squares*, but with the size of each square. The best way to avoid distortion is to not allow the user to draw squares of size bigger than 120.

How about the lower limit? Interestingly, because of the way the "square" procedure works, even a negative value such as -50 works for the flower design! Give it a try!

That means, the flower size can "grow" in the negative direction all the way up to -120.

We can verify that the flower size is within the desired range by checking user's response to the "ask" command. We will ask again and again until "answer" is within the expected range.

Feature Idea # 12: The Field design

Add the "Field" design. This design shows a field of flowers as seen from the sky.

Design:

We already know how to draw a flower. Now, we just need to draw a bunch of them such that:

- Each has a random color
- Each has a random number of petals/squares (within a range of course)
- Each with random petal size (within a range of course)
- Each is placed at a random location on the screen

Does that give you enough hints for how to draw this field of flowers?

Save as Program Version "Advanced"

Congratulations! You have completed all the advanced features of the program. As before, let's save this project.

Compare your program with my program at the link below.

Squares-adv: includes the advanced features listed above.

Link: https://scratch.mit.edu/projects/104974779/

How to run the program:

1. Click on the "Green flag": everything is reset to the original state.
2. Select a design by clicking on one of the buttons.
3. Enter inputs if prompted and watch the design.

Additional Challenge

In feature idea # 11 above, we check the user input to make sure it is within the acceptable range. This is called "input validation". Use such input validation at other places in your program where you get input from the user.

Solutions to Feature Ideas

Feature idea # 1:

Basic script that draws a square of size 100:

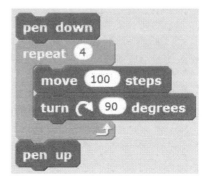

A new procedure called "square":

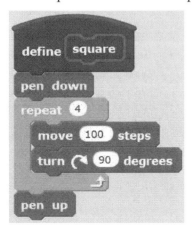

The final procedure script, with an input called "length":

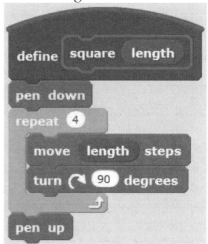

Feature idea # 2:

Here is the final script. It draws 20 squares when you press the S key. By modifying the input of "repeat" you can draw as many squares as you want.

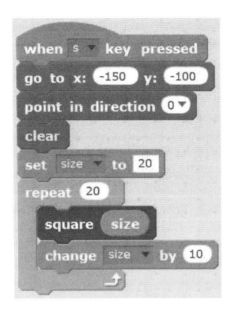

Feature idea # 3:

As expected, this script does the needful!

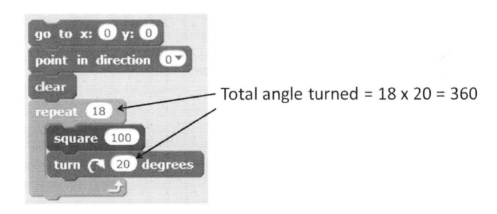

Total angle turned = 18 x 20 = 360

Feature idea # 4:

Here is the final script. It draws a tunnel of 10 squares. By changing the input of "repeat" we can draw as many squares as we want.

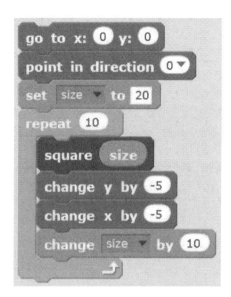

Feature idea # 5:

Script for the shell design:

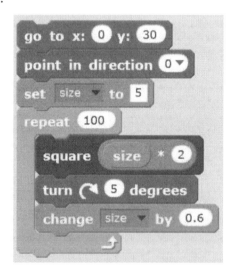

Feature idea # 6:

The solution is given in the design section itself.

Feature idea # 7:

The solution is given in the design section itself.

Feature idea # 8:

The following script for the "Tunnel" button sends such a broadcast:

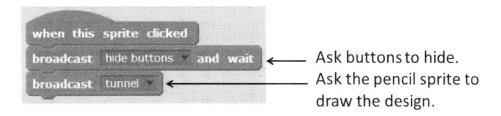

Ask buttons to hide.
Ask the pencil sprite to draw the design.

Feature idea # 9:

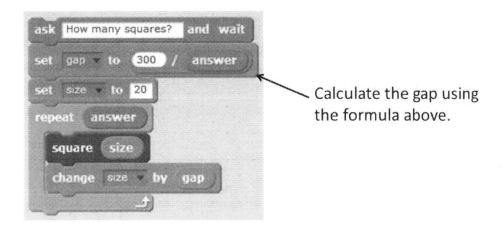

Calculate the gap using the formula above.

Feature idea # 10:

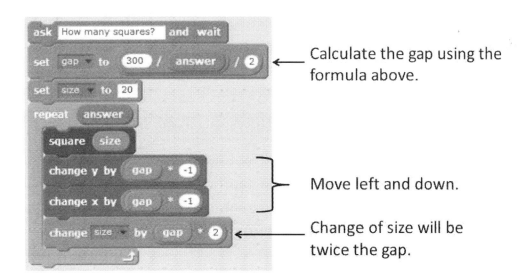

Calculate the gap using the formula above.

Move left and down.

Change of size will be twice the gap.

Feature idea # 11:

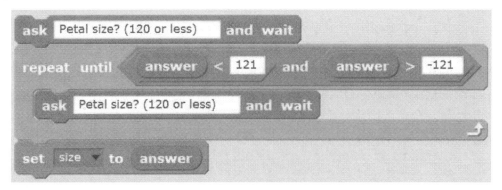

Feature idea # 12:

This script draws 20 flowers.

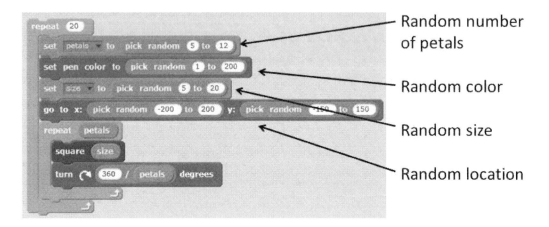

Random number of petals

Random color

Random size

Random location

Design and programming are human activities; forget that and all is lost. — Bjarne Stroustrup

Program Description

The law of optical reflection says that *when a ray of light reflects off a smooth surface (such as a mirror) its angle of incidence is equal to its angle of reflection.* This program will set up a simple interactive experiment to view a demonstration of this law.

A source of light is placed at the top of the screen, and a mirror is placed directly below the light source near the bottom of the screen. When a button is clicked, a ray of light travels from the light source to the mirror and reflects from it. The user can turn the mirror and thus change the angle of incidence of the ray of light.

Check out a working Scratch version of this program. Click on the image below (or the URL just below it). I encourage you to explore the program and its various features. But, don't look at the Scratch scripts yet; we want to design this program ourselves!

How to run the program:

1. Click on the "Green flag": the "help" screen is displayed; read it carefully.
2. Click anywhere to continue.
3. Set the mirror angle using the slider or by using up/down arrow keys.
4. Click the "Emit ray" button to run the simulation.

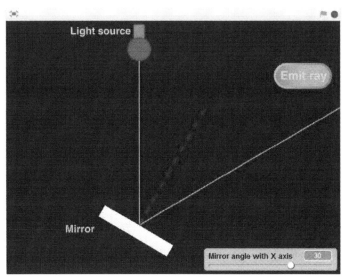

Link: https://scratch.mit.edu/projects/101456673/

Scratch and CS Concepts Used

When we design this program, we will make use of the following Scratch and CS concepts. I assume that you are already familiar with these concepts. If not, or if you want to brush up on these concepts, you should refer to the free downloadable supplement to this book at http://www.abhayjoshi.net/scratch/book1/supplement.pdf.

Main concepts:

- Algorithms
- Arithmetic operators (+, -, *, /)
- Arithmetic expressions
- Conditionals (If-Else)
- Conditionals (IF)
- Conditionals (Wait until)
- Conditionals (nested IF)
- Costumes
- Events
- Looping - simple (repeat, forever)
- Looping - nested
- Motion - absolute
- Random numbers
- Relational operators (=, <, >)
- Sounds - playing sounds
- Synchronization using broadcasting
- User events (mouse)
- User input (buttons)
- Variables - lists
- Variables - numbers
- Variables - strings
- Variables - properties (built-in)
- Variables - local/global scope
- XY Geometry

Additional concepts (for the advanced version):

- OOP - creating instances using clones

High Level Design

Let's look at the main screen of the program and try to point out the different pieces.

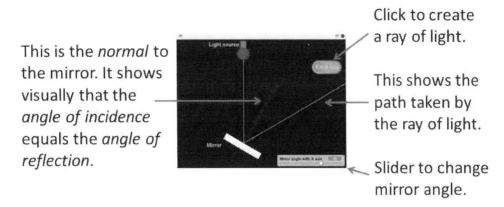

Click to create a ray of light.

This is the *normal* to the mirror. It shows visually that the *angle of incidence* equals the *angle of reflection.*

This shows the path taken by the ray of light.

Slider to change mirror angle.

The order in which we should work on these different pieces of the program is really up to us. We should probably first draw the sprites for the light source and the mirror, use the arrow keys to rotate the mirror, draw a light ray emanating from the bulb and reflecting off the mirror, and use a button to cause the ray of light to be emitted.

In the next version, we will calculate the reflection angle properly (according to laws of optics), control the mirror angle remotely, and demonstrate to the user that the reflection is actually symmetric. We will also add niceties such as an arrow showing the direction of the light ray and a bulb flash every time a ray is created.

In the final version, we will put constraints on how much the mirror can be rotated, add a help screen and sounds, and fix a couple of other issues.

So, let's get rolling with these various ideas one by one. Be sure to try writing your own scripts for each idea before looking up the "Solutions" section.

Initial Version

In the initial version of the program, we will work on the following feature ideas:
1. Draw sprites for the light source and the mirror and use the up/down arrow keys to turn the mirror.
2. Draw a light ray emanating from the bulb and reflecting off the mirror (at some arbitrary angle), and use a button to cause a ray of light to be emitted.

For this initial version, give your project a special name (using "Save as"). For example, I am calling my copy as Reflection-1.

Feature Idea # 1: Light and mirror

Draw sprites for the light source and mirror and use up/down arrow keys to turn the mirror.

Design:

I think this is so easy you can do this without any help. Place the light source near the top and the mirror near the bottom but exactly below the light source.

Write scripts such that the *up arrow* turns the mirror left and the *down arrow* turns it right.

Feature Idea # 2: Ray of light

When a button is clicked a light ray should emanate from the bulb and reflect off the mirror (at some arbitrary angle for now).

<u>Step 1</u>: Draw a light ray emanating from the bulb and reflecting off the mirror (at some arbitrary angle).

Design:

The idea is this: when signaled a line should be drawn starting from the light bulb going straight down to the mirror and reflecting off it.

We will need to use a new sprite to do this drawing. We will call it "photon" since it shows the path of light. It should be really tiny since we don't need to see it, but, at the same time, it can't be hidden because it needs to sense touching the mirror.

We want to show the ray traveling slowly (since it's a simulation), and the ray only needs to travel a finite distance (from the bulb to the mirror and then to one of the screen edges). So, we can use a repeat loop for the motion of the photon sprite.

The algorithm this sprite will follow will be as follows:

```
Go to the light source
Point towards the mirror
Pen down
Repeat N
  If touching mirror
    Turn 150  ←——————————
  End-if
  Move short distance
End-repeat
```

This angle is completely arbitrary. You can use any number you want.

Design:

This is quite straightforward. Have a button sprite, which, when clicked, will send a message to the "photon" sprite to initiate the ray of light.

Save as Program Version 1

Before continuing to the next set of ideas, we will save our project. This way, we have a backup of our project that we can go back to if required for any reason.

Compare your program with my program at the link below.

Reflection-1: includes ideas 1 and 2 explained above.

Link: https://scratch.mit.edu/projects/101456512/

How to run the program:
1. Click on the "Green flag": the mirror becomes horizontal.
2. Set the mirror angle using the up/down arrow keys.
3. Click the "Emit ray" button to run the simulation.

Next Set of Features/ideas:
1. Calculate the angle of reflection properly (according to the laws of optics).
2. Allow the user to control the angle of the mirror (in addition to using the arrow keys).
3. Show visually that the reflection is actually symmetric around the normal.
4. Add niceties such as an arrow showing the direction of the light ray and a flash of the bulb every time a ray is created.

For this version, make a copy of your project (using "Save as") under a different name. For example, I am calling my copy as Reflection-2.

Feature Idea # 3: Angle of reflection

Right now the ray of light reflects at an arbitrary angle. Calculate the angle properly (according to the law of reflection).

Design:

The following figure shows how the ray would actually reflect according to the laws of optics. The letters indicate various angles.

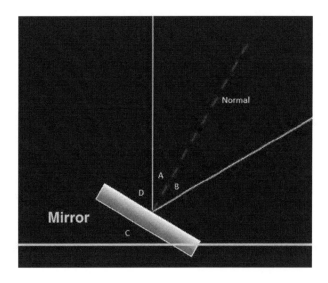

Notes:
1. "Normal" is a line that is perpendicular to the mirror.
2. *A* is the angle of incidence, i.e. the angle of the incoming ray with the normal.
3. *B* is the angle of reflection, i.e. the angle of the outgoing ray with the normal.
4. *C* is the angle made by the mirror with the X-axis.
5. *D* is the angle made by the ray with the mirror.
6. According to laws of optics, A=B.

The figure above and the adjoining notes explain how things work according to the law of reflection.

Using our knowledge of Geometry, we can see that:

A + D = C + D = 90
So, A = C

We can find out C using the mirror's "direction" property. And thus, we will know the other angles. The following *modified* algorithm shows how we can use this information to reflect the ray of light correctly. Note the boldface lines.

```
Go to the light source
Point towards the mirror
Pen down
A = "direction" of mirror
Repeat N
  If touching mirror
    Point in direction = 2 * A
  End-if
  Move short distance
End-repeat
```

Feature Idea # 4: Control mirror angle

Provide a feature to remotely control the angle of the mirror. It should also allow the user to know the value of the angle.

Design:

Right now, we are using the arrow keys to turn the mirror. What other mechanism can you use to turn the mirror remotely? Think of this as a problem of changing its angle with the X axis.

We can use a *slider variable* to achieve this: the mirror sprite will continuously track the value of the variable. So, if the user changes the value of the variable it will immediately cause the mirror to turn.

In turn, we will also need to modify the arrow scripts to ensure the variable is updated when the mirror is turned using the arrow keys. See if you can modify your scripts to implement this idea.

Feature Idea # 5: Explain reflection

Demonstrate to the user visually that the reflection is symmetric, i.e. the ray of light makes the same angle with the normal before and after reflection.

Design:

This is a simple matter of drawing a normal (line perpendicular to the mirror) which will indicate visually that the law of reflection is obeyed by the light ray.

Once again, we will need a new sprite (we will call it "normal") to draw the normal – in this case a dotted line so that it contrasts with the ray of light. This sprite can really be anything since it can do the drawing while staying hidden. After drawing the normal, we can display a text message to reinforce that the two angles are identical. Here is the algorithm that will do the job:

```
Go to the center of the mirror
Point in direction of the mirror
Repeat 10
    Pen down  ┐
    Move 10   │
    Pen up    ├─ This loop draws the dashed line.
    Move 10   ┘
End-repeat          This can be implemented by sending
Display text message     a message to another text sprite that will
                         then become visible.
```

Feature Idea # 6: Arrow and flash

Add niceties such as an arrow showing the direction of the light ray as it travels, and a flash of the bulb every time a ray is created.

Step 1: *Using an arrow show the path taken by the ray of light.*

Design:

This is a simple matter of having an "arrow" sprite piggybacking the "photon" sprite as it draws the path of the ray of light. This should be an appropriately sized arrow that will continuously track the position and direction of the "photon" sprite.

Step 2: *Flash the bulb every time a ray is created.*

Design:

This is a simple matter of having another costume for the light bulb with a lighter color and then showing a quick switch of costumes every time the "Emit ray" button is clicked.

Save as Program Version 2

Before continuing to the next set of ideas, we will save our project. This way, we have a backup of our project that we can go back to if required for any reason.

Compare your program with my program at the link below.

Reflection-2: includes ideas 3 thru 6 explained above.

Link: https://scratch.mit.edu/projects/101456569/

How to run the program:

1.   Click on the "Green flag": the mirror becomes horizontal.
2.   Set the mirror angle using the slider or by using up/down arrow keys.
3.   Click the "Emit ray" button to run the simulation.

Final Set of Features/ideas:

1. It doesn't make sense to turn the mirror beyond its reflecting surface. Put constraints on how much the mirror can be rotated.
2. Add a help screen and sounds.
3. Stop drawing the light ray after reaching the screen edges.

For this final version, make a copy of your project (using "Save as") under a different name. For example, I am calling my copy as Reflection-final.

Feature Idea # 7: Mirror constraints

Put constraints on how much the mirror can be rotated. It doesn't make sense to rotate it more than 90 degrees on either side.

Design:

We already have the variable "Mirror angle with the X axis" which at all times shows and also *controls* the mirror angle. Can you use this variable to impose these constraints?

Yes, we can add checks to ensure that the value of this variable does not go beyond our constraints.

Modify your "mirror" scripts to implement this idea.

Feature Idea # 8: Help and sounds

Add a help screen and suitable sounds.

Design:

We could design a "help" sprite which will come on first when the green flag is clicked. After the user clicks on this sprite the main simulation screen will appear. We will need to replace the "green flag" event that triggers the other sprites by a broadcast event.

See if you can write scripts to implement this idea.

As far as sounds are concerned, you can use them wherever you want. I have used a sound when the ray travels and a sound when it bounces off the mirror.

Feature Idea # 9: Edge detection

Right now our program continues drawing the ray of light even after reaching the edge of the screen. Figure out a way to stop drawing after reaching the screen edges.

Design:

We can use the "touching edge" condition in an IF command to implement this feature. Instead of using a "repeat" loop, we can use the "repeat until" loop.

Modify your "photon" script to implement this idea.

Save as Program Version "Final"

Congratulations! You have completed all the main features of the program. As before, let's save this project before continuing to the advanced ideas.

Compare your program with my program at the link below.

Reflection-final: includes ideas 7 thru 9 explained above.

Link: https://scratch.mit.edu/projects/101456765/

How to run the program:
1.   Click on the "Green flag": the "help" screen is displayed; read it carefully.
2.   Click anywhere to continue.
3.   Set the mirror angle using the slider or by using up/down arrow keys.
4.   Click the "Emit ray" button to run the simulation.

Design Steps – Advanced Version

We can add an additional improvement to our final version as described below. This feature is optional, so, implement only if you find it interesting and useful.

For this advanced version, make a copy of your project (using "Save as") under a different name. For example, I am calling my copy as Reflection-adv.

Feature Idea # 10: Disable emit

Right now our program has a small problem. The "emit ray" button works even after you stop the program by clicking the stop button. This is problematic because the arrow does not show up. Fix this issue.

Design:

Ideally, when the program is stopped, the "emit ray" button should not work. But this is not possible because its script is event-driven and every time you click the button, the script will run.

So, how will you disable the "emit ray" button after the program is stopped?

Here is a hint: instead of disabling, you could simply hide it when the program is not running. Can you think of how that can be managed?

Well, the idea of "clones" comes to rescue. The actual visible button could be a clone – which will disappear as soon as the program has been stopped.

Modify your "emit" scripts to implement this idea.

Save as Program Version "Advanced"

Congratulations! You have completed all the advanced features of the program. As before, let's save this project.

Compare your program with my program at the link below.

Reflection-adv: includes the advanced features listed above.

Link: `https://scratch.mit.edu/projects/101456673/`

How to run the program:

1. Click the "Green flag": the "help" screen is displayed.
2. Click anywhere to continue.
3. Set the mirror angle using the slider or by using up/down keys.
4. Click the "Emit ray" button to run the simulation.

Solutions to Feature Ideas

Feature idea # 1:

Note that I have designed the mirror sprite as shown below:

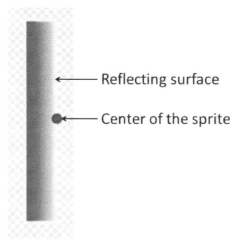

The advantage of drawing it standing up is that, when it is placed flat on the screen (by turning left 90 degrees), its "direction" property will have the value of 0. This is useful later when we do calculations related to the "law of reflection". But, you should feel free to draw the mirror differently if you wish.

The placement of the center of the sprite (as shown above) will help us to align the mirror and the light source properly and to ensure that the ray of light will always touch the same point when the mirror is rotated.

Scripts to turn the mirror sprite:

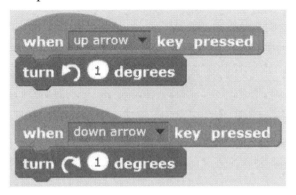

Feature idea # 2:

Step 1:

Script for the "photon" sprite:

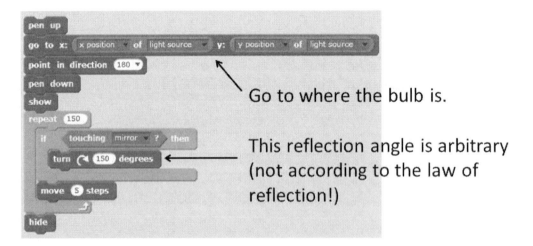

Go to where the bulb is.

This reflection angle is arbitrary (not according to the law of reflection!)

Step 2:

Script for the button sprite:

Event for the photon script:

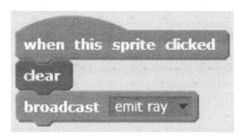

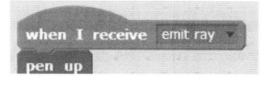

Feature idea # 3:

Modified script for the "photon" sprite:

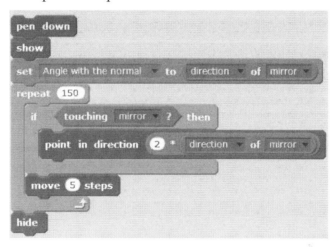

Feature idea # 4:

Arrow scripts of "mirror" sprite:

Remote control script of "mirror" sprite:

Feature idea # 5:

Script for "normal" sprite:

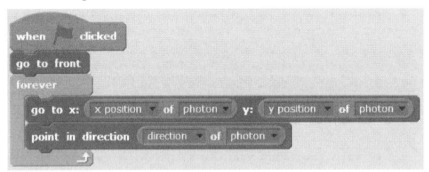

Feature idea # 6:

Step 1:

Script for the "arrow" sprite:

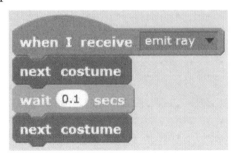

Step 2:

Script for "light source" sprite:

Feature idea # 7:

Scripts for the "mirror" sprite:

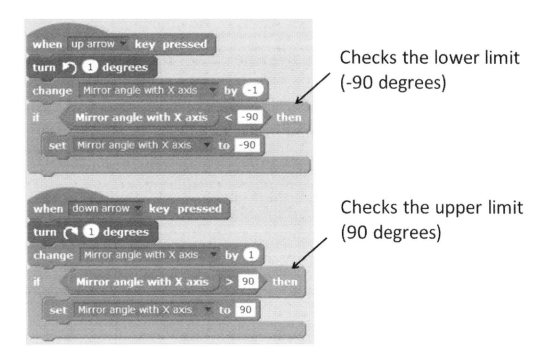

Checks the lower limit
(-90 degrees)

Checks the upper limit
(90 degrees)

Feature idea # 8:

When the help sprite is
clicked it will send a broadcast:

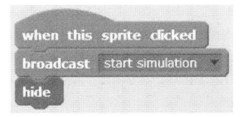

Example of other sprites receiving
this message:

Feature idea # 9:

Snippet of the modified script for the "photon" sprite:

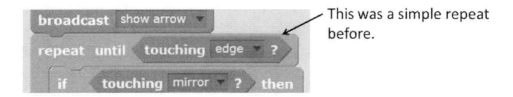

This was a simple repeat before.

Feature idea # 10:

Scripts for the "emit" sprite:

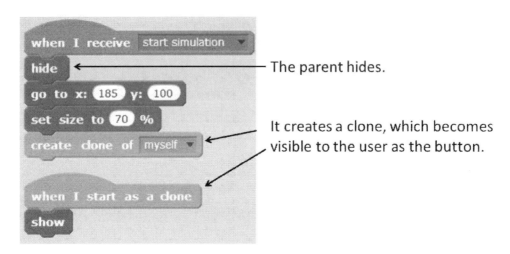

The parent hides.

It creates a clone, which becomes visible to the user as the button.

Controlling complexity is the essence of computer programming. – Brian Kernighan

Project 4: Ping Pong

Program Description

This is a game that two players play with a ball and two flat paddles. The paddles only move up and down. The left paddle belongs to "player1" and it uses the 'w' and 's' keys. The right paddle belongs to "player2" and it uses the up/down arrow keys. When the ball touches either of the left/right edges of the screen the opposing player gets a point.

There are 3 levels of difficulty. In level 1, which is the easiest, the ball moves at a constant speed, which you can set at the beginning of the game. In level 2, the ball speed varies randomly (within certain limits, of course) every time it touches a paddle. The player can set the min and max limits of the ball speed. In level 3, in addition to speed variation, the angle of bounce when the ball touches a paddle also varies (to introduce an element of surprise for the opponent).

The first player to make 11 points wins the game.

Do you want to check out a working Scratch version of this program? Click the image below (or the URL just below it). I encourage you to explore the program and its various features. But, don't look at the Scratch scripts yet; we want to design this program ourselves!

How to run the game:

1. Click the "Green flag": a help screen appears. Read the instructions carefully.
2. Click "Pick level" to select the level of difficulty (1 to 3).
3. For levels 2 and 3, enter the min and max speed for the ball.
4. Click "Start game" to begin playing. If level=1, use the speed 'slider' to set the speed of the ball.
5. Press SPACE BAR to serve.

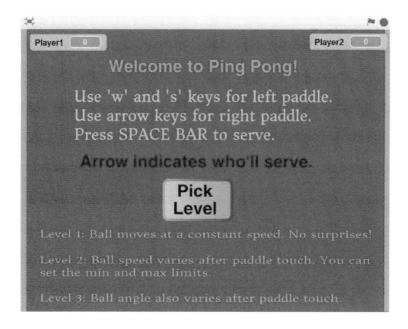

Link: https://scratch.mit.edu/projects/106705607/

Scratch and CS Concepts Used

When we design this program, we will make use of the following Scratch and CS concepts. I assume that you are already familiar with these concepts. If not, or if you want to brush up on these concepts, you should refer to the free downloadable supplement to this book at http://www.abhayjoshi.net/scratch/book1/supplement.pdf.

Main concepts:
- Arithmetic operators (+, -, *, /)
- Backdrops - multiple
- Concurrency - running scripts in parallel
- Conditionals (If-Else)
- Conditionals (IF)
- Conditionals (Wait until)
- Events
- Logic operators (and, or, not)
- Looping - simple (repeat, forever)
- Motion - absolute
- Motion - relative

- Motion - smooth using repeat
- Random numbers
- Relational operators (=, <, >)
- Sensing touch
- Sequence
- Sounds - playing sounds
- Stopping scripts
- Synchronization using broadcasting
- User events (keyboard)
- User events (keyboard - polling)
- User input (buttons)
- Variables - numbers
- Variables - properties (built-in)
- Variables - as remote control
- XY Geometry

Additional concepts (for the advanced version):
- Procedures with inputs
- Looping - conditional (repeat until)
- Motion - direction and bouncing
- User input (ASK)
- User input validation

High Level Design:

This is where we take a step back from the computer (literally!), analyze the problem in our mind (and on a piece of paper if necessary), and break it down into multiple smaller ideas which can be programmed separately.

Let's take a look at the main screen of the game and try to point out the different pieces.

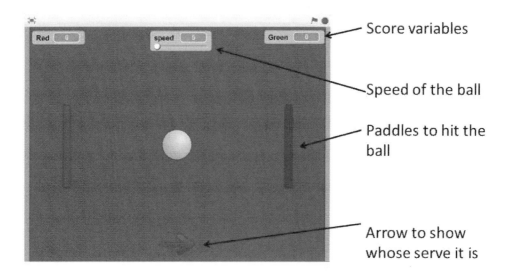

Score variables

Speed of the ball

Paddles to hit the ball

Arrow to show whose serve it is

Initial Set of Features:

Clearly, it makes sense to start setting up the most basic apparatus – which is the ball and the two paddles. The ball will bounce around the screen at a constant speed and also off the paddles. The paddles will move up and down. We can sense touch to detect a miss (when one of the vertical edges is touched). We will keep track of each player's score using variables. And we will use number keys to decide which player will serve. Finally, we will add a help screen and some interesting sounds.

That will be our starting version of the game. We will discuss what to do next after building this version.

For this initial version, give your project a special name (using "Save as"). For example, I am calling my copy as Pingpong-1.

So, let's get rolling with these various ideas one by one. Be sure to try writing your own scripts for each idea before looking up the "Solutions" section.

Feature Idea # 1: The ball sprite

Get a "ball" sprite and make it bounce freely. After pressing SPACE BAR the ball should start bouncing around. Keys "1" and "2" will decide which player will serve the ball.

Design:

I think this is so easy you can straightaway write the scripts.

Feature Idea # 2: The two paddles

Add the two paddles. This involves two steps.

Step 1: The paddles should move up-down only.

Design:

In order to move only vertically, each paddle should only change its Y coordinate. The left paddle will use the 's' and 'w' keys and the right paddle will use the up/down arrows for the movement.

Step 2: Make the ball bounce off the paddles.

Design:

Bouncing off the paddle is straightforward. We can use the "touching" condition in an IF statement. "Bouncing" actually is a complex idea, but for now we will keep it simple: we will assume that bouncing essentially means turning around by some angle and moving away. The turning angle must be large. You can experiment and try different values.

Feature Idea # 3: The Miss

If the ball touches the left or right edge of the screen, it should be treated as a "miss". The game should be paused for a new serve.

Design:

Sensing that the ball has touched the left or the right edge is easy. In order to keep a separate score for each player (we will implement the "score" feature later), it will be good to know which edge the ball has touched. So, it is better if we draw the edges as sprites instead of making them part of the background.

The first step is to draw a colored thick line along each of the left and right edges of the screen.

We will use the "touching" condition in an IF statement to sense touch with these edges. What needs to happen when the ball touches an edge? The game needs to pause for the next serve, i.e. the ball needs to return to the center and stop moving. We can achieve this by using the STOP command and stop all scripts.

Feature Idea # 4: Keeping score

Keep score for each player.

Design:

We can add a variable for each player to count his/her points. We will define a pair of variables called *Red* and *Green* (since the paddles are colored red and green) which will record points for each player.

But, how do we know which player has won a point? Well, we already have a separate script to sense touching each edge (left and right). Each script will detect the touch and increment the appropriate score variable.

Feature Idea # 5: Help screen and sounds

Add a help screen before starting the game, telling the player which keys to use to move the paddles, how to serve, how to set the direction of the serve, etc. Also add sounds for paddles and edges.

Design:

This should be straightforward. In my program I display the help screen when the Green flag is clicked, and pressing the "z" key brings up the game screen. You can check out the scripts in the program below.

Save as Program Version 1

Before continuing to the next set of ideas, we will save our project. This way, we have a backup of our project that we can go back to if required for any reason.

Compare your program with my program at the link below.

Pingpong-1: includes ideas 1 thru 5 explained above.

Link: https://scratch.mit.edu/projects/106705468/

How to run the program:

1. Click the "Green flag": a help screen appears.
2. Press 'z' to start the game.
3. For every serve:
    a. Press '1' or '2' to decide which player should serve.
    b. Press SPACE BAR to serve the ball.

Next Set of Features/ideas:

In our basic version (above) the paddle operation is not satisfactory – it is sluggish and the paddles refuse to move at the same time. We will fix that problem. Next, we will add the feature of declaring when a player wins the game. Instead of pressing a key to change serve, we will make it automatic. Finally we will add an arrow sprite that will indicate whose serve it is.

For this version, make a copy of your project (using "Save as") under a different name. For example, I am calling my copy as Pingpong-2.

Feature Idea # 6: Improved paddle movement

The paddle movement is kind of sluggish. Also, the two paddles refuse to move at the same time. Fix these problems.

Design:

Scratch allows two ways to handle key-press events. One is called "event-driven" which we have already used – using the "When key pressed" block.

The other way is called "polling-driven" which involves continuously checking the state of the key.

The following table shows these two approaches:

Event-driven: Polling-driven:

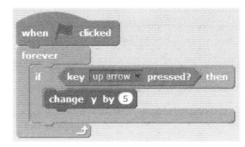

The polling approach is much more responsive than the event-driven approach. The polling approach also allows you to stop the program completely because once the script stops, the key press won't have any effect until the Green Flag is clicked again.

Replace the event-based scripts by scripts based on this new polling-driven approach.

Feature Idea # 7: Declare game over

When one of the players reaches the winning score, stop the game and declare who won.

Design:

Let's say the winning score is 11. This can, of course, be changed easily.

We already have variables *Red* and *Green* that keep track of each player's score. Now, we just have to monitor each of these variables and when one of them exceeds 10, we need to stop the game and change the backdrop to something that declares who won. We could have two separate backdrops – one for Red and one for Green. This script can be owned by the stage.

Feature Idea # 8: Whose serve is it?

Right now the user has to keep track of whose "serve" it is. Make the program keep track of this automatically.

Design:

We already have scripts to tell us which edge was hit by the ball. So, it would be easy to decide who will make the next serve. Let's have another variable called *service* that will keep track of whose serve it is: if it is "1" it's the serve of Red, if it is "2" it's the serve of Green. Depending on the value of *service*, the ball's direction will be set appropriately (which was earlier by done by the player by pressing keys "1" or "2").

Feature Idea # 9: Arrow indicator for serve

This is just a cosmetic change. Include an arrow sprite which will show whose "serve" it is right now.

Design:

We already have the variable *Service* that tells us whose serve it is. We just need to include a new *arrow* sprite which will orient itself according to this variable.

Save as Program Version 2

Before continuing to the next set of ideas, we will save our project. This way, we have a backup of our project that we can go back to if required for any reason.

Compare your program with my program at the link below.

Pingpong-2: includes ideas 6 thru 9 explained above.
Link: https://scratch.mit.edu/projects/106705511/

How to run the program:
1. Click the "Green flag": a help screen appears. Read the instructions carefully.
2. Press 'z' to begin playing.
3. Press SPACE BAR to serve the ball.

Final Set of Features/ideas:

Right now the player has to press the 'z' key to start the game, which is kind of boring. We will replace that with a "Start game" button. Instead of having the ball go at a constant speed, we will provide a slider which will let the player vary the ball speed. In the current version each serve is made at the same angle (which is straight). We will make this a bit unpredictable. Finally, we will try to find an automatic fix for the occasional problem of the ball motion becoming too vertical.

For this final version, make a copy of your project (using "Save as") under a different name. For example, I am calling my copy as Pingpong-final.

Feature Idea # 10: Variable speed

Right now the speed of the ball is fixed. Change this so that the user can vary the speed of the ball.

Design:

The speed of the ball is decided by the "move" command. So, we simply have to substitute a *speed* variable in place of the number. We will display the *speed* variable as a slider so that the player can change its value while playing the game.

See if you can modify your script to implement this idea.

Feature Idea # 11: The Start button

Instead of starting on a key press (the 'z' key) have a Start button to begin play.

Design:

This is actually required since we need to set things up (variables, etc.) before starting the game. When the green flag is clicked, the variables will be initialized to 0 and the help screen, along with the Start button, will be presented. When the user clicks the Start button, a "start game" message will be sent to everyone.

Feature Idea # 12: Random angle for each serve

Right now, the angle of every serve is the same. Make this angle unpredictable to make the game more interesting.

Design:

Unpredictable is the same as "random". Instead of serving straight, i.e. orienting the ball exactly east or west, we should put some randomness in its angle.

This involves modifying the earlier script that orients the ball before each serve. While setting up the serve for player Red, the direction of the ball should be picked randomly from 45 to 135, to ensure player Green has a fighting chance to return the serve. Similarly, while setting up the serve for player Green, the direction of the ball should be picked randomly from -45 to -135.

Feature Idea # 13: Avoid vertical drift

There is a slight problem in our program. Sometimes the ball's direction becomes such that it starts moving more up-down than left-right. The current version allows you to press keys 1 or 2 to make the ball move horizontally again. See if you can make this correction automatic.

Design:

This is not a problem in real-life ping pong because the ball would go out of bounds and one of the players would score a point. But, in our program, we allow the ball to bounce off the top and bottom edges.

How can the program detect that the ball is moving too vertical?

The *direction* property of the ball tells us the ball's angle with North. So, we could monitor this *direction* and ensure it doesn't get too close to 0. For example, we can disallow it to become less than 45 or more than -45.

Note that in our script we cannot just have a condition like "IF direction < 45" because that covers everything from 45 to -180! It is better to say "IF direction < 45 AND direction > 0". Get it?

Save as the Final Program Version

Congratulations! You have completed all the main features of the game. As before, let's save this project before continuing to the advanced ideas.

Compare your program with my program at the link below.

Pingpong-final: includes ideas 9 thru 13 explained above.
Link: https://scratch.mit.edu/projects/106705607/

How to run the program:
1. Click the "Green flag": a help screen appears. Read the instructions carefully.
2. Click "Start game" to begin playing. Use the speed 'slider' to set the speed of the ball.
3. Press SPACE BAR to serve the ball.

Advanced Set of Features/ideas:

The next set of features is optional; implement those you find interesting and useful.

Currently the ball bounces off the paddles pretty arbitrarily. We will use a correct bouncing technique. Next, we will make the game multi-level, i.e. add a couple of levels of challenge.

For this advanced version, make a copy of your project (using "Save as") under a different name. For example, I am calling my copy as Pingpong-adv.

Feature Idea # 14: Bouncing correctly

We have implemented the action of "bouncing" off the paddles quite arbitrarily. Make it more realistic (like the Scratch command "if on edge bounce").

Design:

Bouncing is nothing but changing the direction of motion. In Scratch, the *direction* property (angle with North) of a sprite indicates its direction.

If you want to understand how bouncing works in the command "If on edge bounce", look up the concept "bouncing" in the book's Appendix.

To keep things simple, we will only consider bouncing off the long vertical surfaces of the paddles (and ignore the short horizontal edges). When the ball bounces off a vertical surface its *direction* property changes in sign. So, 30 becomes -30, -80 becomes 80, and so on.

Feature Idea # 15: Multiple levels of difficulty

Right now we have only one level of difficulty – in which the speed of the ball can be varied. Add a couple of more levels of difficulty as suggested below:

In real-life ping pong, players usually hit the ball at different speeds. Add this feature in level 2.

In real-life ping pong, players also hit the ball at different angles. Add this feature in level 3.

<u>Step 1</u>: *Allow the player to choose a level of difficulty at the start of the game.*

Design:

We will use a new variable called *Level* to know the difficulty level the user has chosen.

We could add an additional button called "Pick level" which will allow the player to set this variable. We can use the ASK command for this purpose.

Step 2: Add these levels of difficulty to the ball scripts.

Design:

For level 2, we just need to add a random variation to the _speed_ variable (after it touches a paddle) because that variable decides the speed of the ball.

For level 3, (in addition to the speed change of level 2) we also need to add a random turn to the ball (after it touches a paddle).

Step 3: One problem with the above changes is that it is possible that the speed of the ball can become too large or too small. Set both upper and lower limits.

Design:

We will add two more variables – _minspeed_ and _maxspeed_ which will be the upper and lower limits on the speed. When the user chooses the level of difficulty at the start of the game, we will also ask him to set these limits.

The scripts would be very similar to the one we used above to set the _Level_ variable.

Additional Challenge

If you see the script of the "Pick level" button, there are very similar code snippets repeated to get user input for _level_, _minspeed_, and _maxspeed_. Can you write a procedure (a new Scratch block) called _GetInput_ such that the main script will replace this code?

Save as Program Version "Advanced"

Congratulations! You have completed all the advanced features of the game. As before, let's save this project.

Compare your program with my program at the link below.

Pingpong-adv: includes the advanced features listed above.
Link: https://scratch.mit.edu/projects/106705673/

How to run the program:
1. Click the "Green flag": a help screen appears. Read the instructions carefully.
2. Click "Pick level" to select the level of difficulty (1 to 3).
3. For levels 2 and 3, enter the min and max speed for the ball.
4. Click "Start game" to begin playing. If level=1, use the speed 'slider' to set the speed of the ball.
5. Press SPACE BAR to serve the ball.

Solutions to Feature Ideas

Feature idea # 1:

Scripts for the "Ball" sprite:

Scripts to determine direction of the "serve".

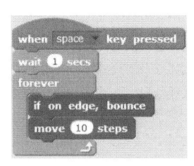

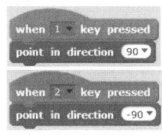

Feature idea # 2:

Step 1: Scripts for the paddles:

Left paddle:

Right paddle:

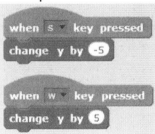

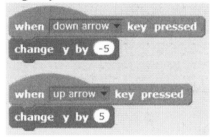

Step 2:

Script for the "ball" sprite to bounce off the _right_ paddle:

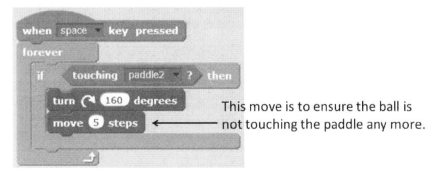

This move is to ensure the ball is not touching the paddle any more.

Feature idea # 3:

Script for the "ball" sprite to sense the *left* edge (there will be a similar script for the *right* edge):

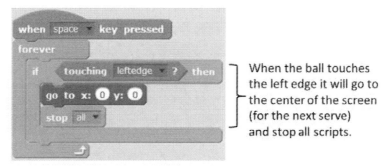

When the ball touches the left edge it will go to the center of the screen (for the next serve) and stop all scripts.

Feature idea # 4:

Modified script for the "ball" sprite that keeps score for player Green:

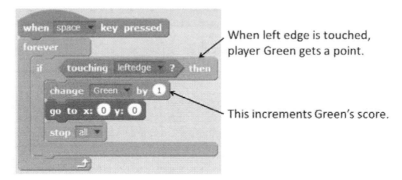

When left edge is touched, player Green gets a point.

This increments Green's score.

Feature idea # 6:

Script for the right paddle is shown here:

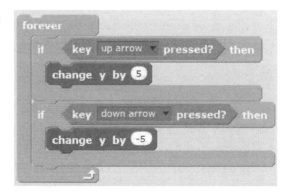

Feature idea # 7:

Stage script for player Green:

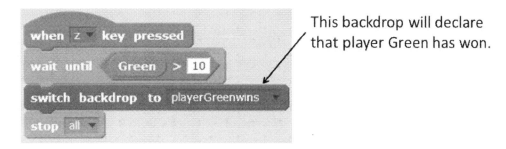

This backdrop will declare that player Green has won.

Feature idea # 8:

Modified ball script that senses the left edge:

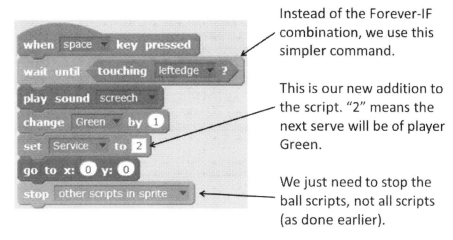

Instead of the Forever-IF combination, we use this simpler command.

This is our new addition to the script. "2" means the next serve will be of player Green.

We just need to stop the ball scripts, not all scripts (as done earlier).

There will be a similar script for the right edge.

The following snippet of a Ball script shows how the "serve" will happen in the correct direction.

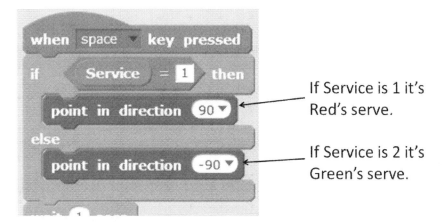

If Service is 1 it's Red's serve.

If Service is 2 it's Green's serve.

Feature idea # 9:

Script for the "arrow" sprite:

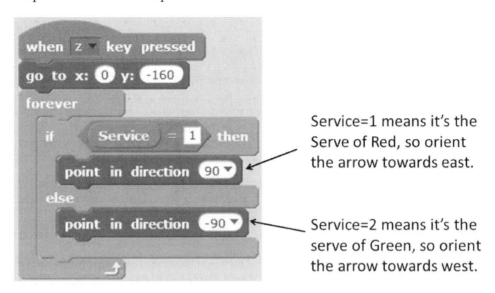

Service=1 means it's the Serve of Red, so orient the arrow towards east.

Service=2 means it's the serve of Green, so orient the arrow towards west.

Feature idea # 10:

Script for the "ball" sprite:

Variable shown as a slider.

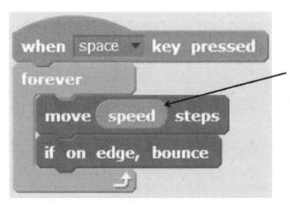

As the value of "speed" changes the actual speed of the sprite will also change.

Feature idea # 11:
See the final program scripts for this feature idea.

Feature idea # 12:
Snippet of the modified ball script:

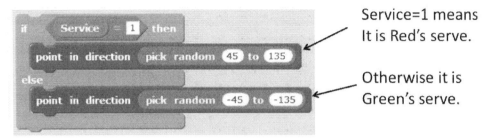

Service=1 means It is Red's serve.

Otherwise it is Green's serve.

Feature idea # 13:
Additional script for the ball sprite:

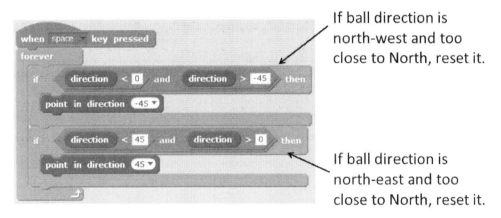

If ball direction is north-west and too close to North, reset it.

If ball direction is north-east and too close to North, reset it.

Feature idea # 14:
Snippet of the modified "ball" script for touching paddles:

To this, we will add a slight randomness to ensure the ball doesn't get stuck in some fixed pattern.

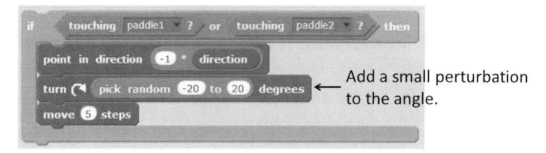

Add a small perturbation to the angle.

Feature idea # 15:

Step 1:

Script for the "Pick level" button sprite:

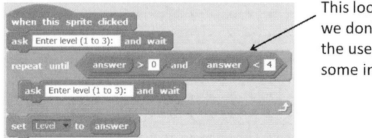

This loop ensures we don't allow the user to enter some incorrect number.

Step 2:

Addition to the "ball" script that senses touch with paddles:

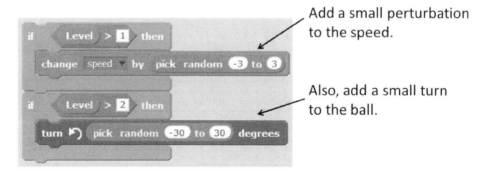

Add a small perturbation to the speed.

Also, add a small turn to the ball.

Step 3:

Check out the scripts in the final program.

Program Description

This is a program in which you design a combination digital-analog clock. The digital clock shows hours, minutes and seconds as numbers, and the analog clock has all three respective hands. The digital clock uses a 24-hour time format, and the analog clock has indicator for AM/PM. The analog clock shows a tick-tock animation synchronized with the motion of the *second-hand*. Every time you stop and start the clock the animation may change. The user can set the clock time by adding or subtracting minutes.

Do you want to check out a working Scratch version of this program? Click on the image below (or the URL just below it). I encourage you to explore the program and its various features. But, don't look at the Scratch scripts yet; we want to design this program ourselves!

How to run the program:

1. Click the "Green flag": you will see the *welcome* screen followed by the *instructions* screen.
2. Click SET if you want to set the clock. The +/- buttons will appear:
   a. Click the +/- buttons once to add/subtract a minute.
   b. Keep the +/- buttons pressed to add/subtract multiple minutes.
3. Click START to start the clock.
4. Click STOP to stop the clock.

Link: https://scratch.mit.edu/projects/103555093/

Scratch and CS Concepts Used

When we design this program, we will make use of the following Scratch and CS concepts. I assume that you are already familiar with these concepts. If not, or if you want to brush up on these concepts, you should refer to the free downloadable supplement to this book at http://www.abhayjoshi.net/scratch/book1/supplement.pdf.

Main concepts:

- Algorithm
- Arithmetic operators (+, -, *, /)
- Arithmetic expressions
- Backdrops - multiple
- Conditionals (IF and If-Else)
- Conditionals (nested IF)
- Costumes
- Events
- Geometry - square, circle, triangle, spiral
- Logic operators (and, or, not)
- Looping - simple (repeat, forever)
- Looping - conditional (repeat until)
- Motion – absolute and relative
- Motion - smooth using repeat
- Pen commands
- Procedures
- Random numbers
- Relational operators (=, <, >)
- Sequence
- Sounds - playing sounds
- Stopping scripts
- Synchronization using broadcasting
- User events (mouse)
- User events (mouse - polling)
- User input (buttons)
- Variables - numbers
- Variables - properties (built-in)
- Variables - as remote control
- XY Geometry

High Level Design:

Note that we will use a 24-hour format for the digital clock. So, for example, 2:30 am will be shown as 2 hours 30 minutes, and 2:30 pm will be shown as 14 hours 30 minutes.

Let's take a look at the main screen of the program and try to point out the different pieces.

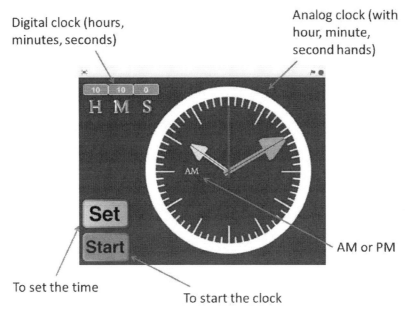

Digital clock (hours, minutes, seconds)

Analog clock (with hour, minute, second hands)

AM or PM

To set the time

To start the clock

The following flow of operations in this program will give us further idea of the different parts that we need to design:
- After the welcome and instructions screens the above screen appears.
- Clicking "Set" brings up two buttons: + and – :
  - Clicking the +/- buttons once adds or subtracts a minute.
  - Keeping the +/- buttons pressed adds or subtracts multiple minutes.
- Clicking "Start" starts the clock and the "stop" button appears.
- Clicking "Stop" button stops the clock and the "start" button appears.

The order in which we should work on these different pieces of the program is really up to us. It probably makes sense to first figure out how to display both the clocks. We will design the analog clock using the pen commands and use sprites for the hands. For the digital clock we just need to use variables.

In the next version, we will tackle the challenge of running the clock and moving the hands correctly. The digital clock will of course be in sync with the analog clock.

In the following version, we will add start/stop buttons to start and stop the clock. More importantly, we will add the facility of setting the time. This will be done through buttons that will allow adding or subtracting minutes.

In the final version, we will add niceties such as an AM/PM indicator, a bell for the strike of hour, tick-tock animations, and welcome/help screens.

So, let's get rolling with these various ideas one by one. Be sure to try writing your own scripts for each idea before looking up the "Solutions" section.

Initial Version

In the initial version of the program, we will work on the following feature ideas:
1. Displaying a digital clock.
2. Drawing the frame of the analog clock.
3. Arranging the hands of the analog clock.
4. Setting a time.

For this initial version, give your project a special name (using "Save as"). For example, I am calling my copy as Clock-1.

Feature Idea # 1: Digital clock
Display a digital clock with hours, minutes, and seconds.

Design:
As you might guess, the digital clock is simply a collection of 3 variables: we will call them H, M, and S to represent hours, minutes, and seconds respectively. We will add labels below them to indicate what each of them is for. And finally, we will simply ask the user for their initial values. This script could be owned by the stage.

Feature Idea # 2: Draw analog clock
Draw the frame of the analog clock with hour and minute markings.

We will use the pen capability to draw everything. We could use any sprite for this purpose since the sprite will stay hidden while doing all the drawing.

As you can see clearly, there are two parts to the frame: the circular border and the markings for minutes and hours. Let's take these one by one.

Step 1: Draw the circular frame.

Design:

How do you draw a circle in Scratch?

A repeated combination of *move* and *turn* will draw a circle if we turn a total of 360 degrees. For example, the code below will draw a circle of length 900 (180 times 5).

```
Repeat 180
   Move 5
   Turn 2
End-repeat
```

We would like to draw a frame that will fit on the screen. The Scratch screen dimensions are 480 x 360, so a circle of diameter 300 will fit easily. A diameter of 300 means a circle of circumference 300 x pi = 300 x 3.14159 = 945, which can be drawn by the code below:

starting point
of the circle

```
Go to x = -100, y = 0

Repeat 180          180 x 5.25 = 945
   Move 5.25        (circumference)
   Turn 2
End-repeat
```

Step 2: Draw the markings for minutes.

Design:

There are 60 minutes and hence 60 short markings on the clock. Each marking is basically a short line segment starting on the circle's circumference going towards its center. If all these markings were extended all the way to the center, what would be the angle between each pair of markings?

Well, that would be 360/60 = 6 degrees. So, we could do the following to draw these 60 markings, right?

```
Repeat 60
   Draw a short line from the circle towards its center
   Turn 6
End-repeat
```

The question is how do we "draw a short line" in step 1? Any suggestions?

Well, this is what we could do. We could draw each line from the center all the way to the circle such that it is partly blank and partly visible. Do you get the idea?

The following algorithm gives a bit more detail. Note that:
M + N = R (radius of the circle)

```
Go to circle's center
Point up (0 degrees)
Repeat 60
    Pen up        ⎤  Draw a blank line.
    Move M        ⎦
    Pen down      ⎤  Draw a short visible line
    Move N        ⎦  (that's our marking)
    Pen up        ⎤  Jump back to the center
    Move -R       ⎦
    Turn 6
End-repeat
```

Step 3: *Draw the hour markings.*

Design:
There are 12 hours and hence 12 hour markings on the clock. These are slightly longer than the markings for minutes. We can use exactly the same technique we used above for drawing markings for minutes, right? Instead of 60 markings we need to draw 12.

Feature Idea # 3: Clock hands
Design and arrange the hour, minute, and second-hands of the analog clock.

Step 1: *Design and place the hands such that they all hang together at the clock's center.*

Design:
This is a matter of designing the 3 hands and arranging them so that they appear as if they are nailed to the center of the clock. Also, when turned they must turn around the point where they are nailed.

Go ahead and design your own hour, minute, and second hands. As per convention, the hour-hand is thick and short, the minute-hand is thick and long, and the second-hand is thin and the longest. Also, design them in the horizontal positions (that is, *flat* instead of *standing*). Why? Because, that way, when their direction is 0 they will align along the 12 o'clock position of the clock.

For example, see the following hour-hand sprite:

Center of the sprite

Sprite is lying flat.

Placement of the hands is slightly tricky. How will you ensure that they are nailed to the clock's center?

Well, it's not all that difficult. Ensure that the center of each hand is somewhere near its left end, and then just use the "Go to x, y" command to make the hand jump to the clock's center. Now, if you turn the hand (using the *turn* command), it will turn around the clock's center as desired.

Step 2: *Set the hands according to the time (as set on the digital clock).*

Design:

In feature-idea #1 we already set the digital clock to a time supplied by the user. Now, we need to ensure that the analog clock shows the same time. We have variables H, M, and S which contain the hours, minutes, and seconds respectively. To keep things simple, let's set S = 0.

How will you arrange the hour-hand and the minute-hand based on the values of H and M? You will need to calculate the angles of these hands with 12 o'clock.

Well, here is the calculation for the minute-hand. For a total of 60 minutes the minute-hand turns 360 degrees. So, for 1 minute, it would turn 360/60=6 degrees. So, for M minutes, the direction of the minute-hand would be M*6 degrees.

How about the hour-hand?

Let's see. There are 12 hours in the clock, which means the hour-hand moves 360 degrees in 12 hours. That means, in one hour the hand will move 360/12 = 30 degrees. That means, in one minute the hour-hand will move 30/60 = 0.5 degrees. So, the total angle of the hour-hand for H hours and M minutes will be: M * 0.5 + H * 30 degrees.

For example, if the time is 1:30, the hour hand will make an angle of 1*30 + 30*0.5 = 45 degrees with 12 o'clock. Does that seem reasonable if you look at the clock at 1:30?

Save as Program Version 1

Before continuing to the next set of ideas, we will save our project. This way, we have a backup of our project that we can go back to if required for any reason.

Compare your program with my program at the link below.

Clock-1: includes ideas 1, 2, and 3 explained above.
Link: https://scratch.mit.edu/projects/103548608/

How to run the program:
1. Click the "Green flag" to start the program.
2. When prompted, enter the time: hours and minutes.
3. The digital and analog clocks are displayed showing the given time.

Next Set of Features/ideas:

As of now, we have a clock without battery, i.e. it doesn't run yet! In this version, we will try to put life into it. We will work on the following features:
1. Starting the clock
2. Running the clock
3. Moving the hands
4. Avoiding overflow/underflow (going below 0 and above 24)

For this version, make a copy of your project (using "Save as") under a different name. For example, I am calling my copy as Clock-2.

Feature Idea # 4: Run the clock
Run both the analog and digital clocks.

Design:
Right now our clocks are set up properly, but we need to make them run like normal clocks, i.e. tick-tock-tick-tock ...

The most basic unit of the clock is one second. Every second, the second-hand should turn and the variable "seconds" should increase by 1. After 60 seconds, the second-hand should complete a full 360 degree revolution. At this time, a minute is completed, which means the variable "minutes" should increase by 1 and the minute-hand should turn a little. After 60 such minutes, the minute-hand should complete a full 360 degree revolution; the variable "hours" should increase by 1 and the hour-hand should turn a little. Finally, after 12 such hours, the hour-hand should complete a full 360 degree revolution. And the cycle should repeat forever.

That is how a clock works. How will you implement it in your program?

Well, as usual, let's go step by step.

Step 1: Take care of counting seconds.

Design:
The following algorithm shows what the second-hand should do:

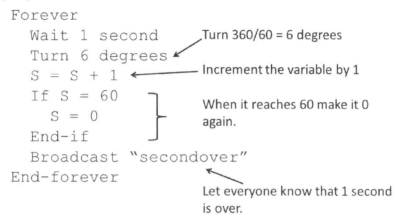

```
Forever
    Wait 1 second          Turn 360/60 = 6 degrees
    Turn 6 degrees ←
    S = S + 1 ←────────── Increment the variable by 1
    If S = 60
        S = 0              When it reaches 60 make it 0
    End-if                 again.
    Broadcast "secondover"
End-forever
                           Let everyone know that 1 second
                           is over.
```

Step 2: Take care of counting minutes.

Design:
To keep things simple, we will move the minute-hand only when 1 minute is over. The following algorithm signals that 1 minute is over:

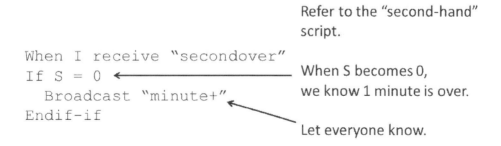

```
                                    Refer to the "second-hand"
                                    script.

When I receive "secondover"
    If S = 0 ←──────────────── When S becomes 0,
        Broadcast "minute+"       we know 1 minute is over.
    Endif-if
                                Let everyone know.
```

At this time, the minute-hand should turn a little and increment the *minutes* variable. See below:

```
When "minute+" is received:
Turn 6 degrees ← Turn 360/60 = 6 degrees
M = M + 1 ←
If M = 60            Increase number of minutes by 1.
    M = 0
                     When it reaches 60, reset it 0 again.
End-if
```

Step 3: *Take care of counting hours.*

Design:

The hour-hand turns a little every time a minute is over. Can you calculate how much it will turn?

Let's see. There are 12 hours in the clock, which means the hour-hand moves 360 degrees in 12 hours. That means, in one hour the hand will move 360/12 = 30 degrees. That means, in one minute the hour-hand will move 30/60 = 0.5 degrees.

So, here is the algorithm for the hour-hand:

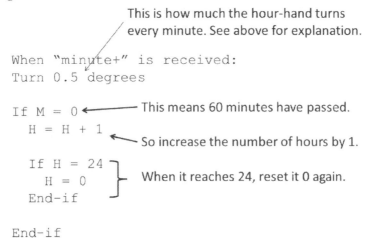

```
                        This is how much the hour-hand turns
                        every minute. See above for explanation.
When "minute+" is received:
Turn 0.5 degrees

If M = 0 ←──────── This means 60 minutes have passed.
    H = H + 1
                  ←──── So increase the number of hours by 1.
    If H = 24
        H = 0          When it reaches 24, reset it 0 again.
    End-if

End-if
```

Save as Program Version 2

Before continuing to the next set of ideas, we will save our project. This way, we have a backup of our project that we can go back to if required for any reason.

Compare your program with my program at the link below.

Clock-2: includes idea 4 explained above.
Link: https://scratch.mit.edu/projects/103548693/

How to run the program:
1. Click on the "Green flag" to start the program.
2. When prompted, enter the initial time: hours and minutes.
3. The clock starts running immediately.

Next Set of Features/ideas:
We will first add two buttons to start and stop the clocks. Next, we will add the capability to set the time by adding or subtracting minutes to the current time.

For this version, make a copy of your project (using "Save as") under a different name. For example, I am calling my copy as Clock-3.

Feature Idea # 5: Start/stop buttons
Add buttons to start and stop the clocks.

Design:
Right now the clock starts as soon as the user enters the initial time. We will replace this by a "start" button, and also add a "stop" button so that the user can stop the clock any time.

Step 1: Add a start button to start the clock.

Design:
This should be quite straightforward. Instead of the stage sending the *startclock* message, we will have a new "start" button sprite do that job. The following script for the start button will do the needful:

Step 2: Add a stop button to stop the clock.

Design:

The "stop" button should become visible when the clock is running. When it is clicked, the clock should stop running and then the "start" button should become visible once again.

Let's first take care of the "start" and "stop" buttons showing up alternately. How will you achieve that?

There are many ways to do this, but, we will do it by switching costumes. So, the "start" button will have a costume for the "stop" button. Can you work out the script for this costume change?

Hint: You can use the built-in Scratch property called "costume #".

Here is the algorithm:

```
When sprite clicked:
If costume# = 1
   Broadcast "startclock"
Else
   Broadcast "stopclock"
Endif
Next costume
```

Step 3: When the "stop" button is clicked the clocks should actually stop running.

Design:

We know that the "forever" loop in the "second-hand" sprite drives everything. So, if we stop the script containing this loop, the clocks will stop.

Feature Idea # 6: Set time

Add a feature to set the clock any time.

Design:

Right now our clock gets set only once in the beginning and there is no way to change the time afterwards. We will add a "set" button which will allow this capability. This button should become visible every time the user stops the clock.

Adding a button sprite is quite easy, and you can do it without any help. Basically this button will send some message when it is clicked and its job is done!

Here is what the scripts of the "set" button will look like:

Show initially and later when the clock is stopped

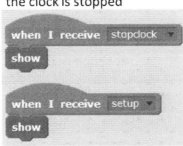

Hide when the clock starts running

When clicked send a message and hide

The real challenge is to figure out how to actually set the clock.

If you have ever used analog clocks, you might remember that they are set by turning the minute-hand. As the minute-hand turns the hour-hand also turns proportionately.

We will use a similar strategy to set our clocks. We will add two new buttons labelled "+" and "–". They will add or subtract a minute when clicked once. And if the user keeps them pressed (i.e. keeps the mouse pointer pressed on them) multiple minutes will be added or subtracted. The minute and hour hands will turn accordingly and the variables H and M will also change accordingly.

Can you work out how to implement this new "+" and "–" feature?

Once again, let's do it step by step.

Step 1: *Add a button "+" which, when clicked, will add one minute to the clock.*

Design:
If you look carefully, you will notice that we already have a script for the "minutes" sprite that adds a minute to the time after receiving the message "minute+". So, the "+" button could also send a "minute+" message to add a minute, right?

Go ahead and design a new "+" button sprite. This button should become visible when the "set" button is clicked and hide when the "start" button is clicked.

Write your scripts to implement this idea.

Step 2: Add a button "–" which, when clicked, will subtract one minute from the clock.

Design:

Along the lines of the "minute+" script which adds a minute to the clock, we could write a "minute-" script to subtract a minute. Note that both the minute and hour hands have the "minute+" script, so, they will both require the "minute-" script.

Can you work out the steps of this new script first for the minute-hand?

Here is how it will work:

```
When I receive "minute-":
Turn left 6 degrees
M = M - 1
```

There is a small problem in this script. Do you see it?

When M = 0, the above script will make it -1, which is not valid, is it? Can you fix this problem and rewrite the script?

Here is how it will look with the fix:

```
When I receive "minute-":
Turn left 6 degrees
M = M - 1
If M = -1
  M = 59
End-if
```

Now, how about the "minute-" script for the hour-hand? Can you work out the steps?

Here is how it will work. If the minute-hand crosses the 0 mark, the hours must go down by 1.

```
When I receive "minute-":
Turn left 0.5 degrees
If M = 59
  H = H - 1
Endif
```

Once again, there is a small problem with this script. Do you see it?

When H = 0, the above script will make it -1, which is invalid. How to fix that?

Here is the final script:

```
When I receive "minute-":
Turn left 0.5 degrees
If M = 59
  H = H - 1
  If H = -1
    H = 23
  Endif
Endif
```

Ok, now write your own scripts for the "–" button, and the "minute-"scripts for the minute and hour hands.

Step 3: Changing just by a minute at a time is quite tedious. Modify the +/- buttons so that they add/subtract multiple minutes if the user keeps them pressed (instead of clicking).

Design:

First, we need to sense when the user keeps the pointer button pressed.

Based on your knowledge of Scratch input events (for the mouse pointer) can you suggest an idea to sense when the pointer button is pressed (instead of clicked)?

Hint: You could use the "mouse down?" event. This event tells you that the mouse button is down (i.e. pressed). So you could have a loop which runs as long as this event is true. In other words, the loop would terminate when this event is NOT true.

And, what should this loop do? Well, that's straightforward. It should repeatedly send the "minute+" or "minute-" messages (depending on which button is pressed).

Save as Program Version 3

Before continuing to the next set of ideas, we will save our project. This way, we have a backup of our project that we can go back to if required for any reason.

Compare your program with my program at the link below.

Clock-3: includes ideas 5 and 6 explained above.
Link: https://scratch.mit.edu/projects/103548794/

How to run the program:
1. Click the "Green flag" to start the program.
2. Click SET if you want to set the clock. The +/- buttons will appear:

a. Click the +/- buttons once to add or subtract a minute.

b. Keep the +/- buttons pressed to add or subtract multiple minutes.

3. Click START to start the clock.

4. Click STOP to stop the clock.

Final Set of Features/ideas:

Next, we will add other niceties as listed below:

1. Checking/setting the AM/PM indicator.
2. Welcome/help screens
3. Bell sound when the hour strikes
4. Tick-tock animation

For this final version, make a copy of your project (using "Save as") under a different name. For example, I am calling my copy as Clock-final.

Feature Idea # 7: Welcome and Help

Add a welcome screen and also a help screen.

Design:

Design a welcome screen and a help screen with instructions on how to use the program.

Step 1: Add a "welcome" screen.

Design:

We will design a new backdrop with appropriate welcome text. This backdrop will appear when the Green flag is clicked. Obviously all other sprites (and variables) will need to hide while this screen is up.

Step 2: Add a "help" screen.

Design:

The help screen can be another backdrop and it will show up when the user clicks anywhere on the "welcome" screen. The stage will thus have 3 backdrops: welcome, help, and clock (a blank backdrop for the actual clock).

How will you design your stage script such that these screens will appear at appropriate times?

Hint: You can use the "backdrop #" property to know which backdrop is up. There is nothing to be done (except changing to the next backdrop) until the final "clock" backdrop appears.

Feature Idea # 8: Show AM/PM

The digital clock uses the 24-hour format so it doesn't need AM/PM. But the analog clock does. Add this feature.

Design:

We could use a sprite with 2 costumes indicating AM and PM. The "hour-hand" knows whenever AM changes to PM and vice versa. So, it could send a message accordingly.

AM is from 0:00 to 11:59 and PM is from 12:00 to 23:59. The following algorithm can be used to check if it's AM or PM:

```
If H < 12
    Broadcast "AM" // It's AM
Else
    Broadcast "PM" // It's PM
End
```

We can make this into a procedure, which can be called every time a minute is added or subtracted.

Feature Idea # 9: Bell toll

Similar to the big wall-clocks make your clock sound a bell when the hour strikes.

Design:

This is quite simple. You just need to play a sound every time an hour is completed. This code would go into the "minute+" script of the hour-hand.

There is a small problem here. The "minute+" script is also used when we are trying the set time. That means, the hour bell would ring even during setting. We don't want that, do we?

How will you fix this problem?

One way is to use a variable called *running* which will tell us if the clock is currently running or not. If running=YES we will ring the bell, if running=NO we will not ring the bell.

And who will set this variable? Well, it makes sense to have the "start" sprite do it since it knows when the program starts and stops.

Feature Idea # 10: Tick-tock animation

Add animations that will run in sync with the second hand.

Design:

This is quite simple. You just need to create a simple two-costume animation that will cycle at the same speed as the second-hand. To make this more interesting, we could have a bunch of animations and pick one of them randomly each time the clock is started.

How will you select an animation using the random function?

Let's say we have 3 possible animations to choose from. "Pick random 1 to 3" will give us a number, which we can store in a variable. The animation sprites will then check the value of this variable to decide whose turn it is to show up. Others will stay hidden.

Save as Program Version "Final"

Congratulations! You have completed all the main features of the program. As before, let's save this project.

Compare your program with my program at the link below.

Clock-final: includes ideas 7 thru 10 explained above.
Link: https://scratch.mit.edu/projects/103555093/

How to run the program:

1. Click the "Green flag": you will see the *welcome* screen followed by the *instructions* screen.
2. Click "Set" if you want to set the clock. The +/- buttons will appear:
   a. Click the +/- buttons once to add or subtract a minute.
   b. Keep the +/- buttons pressed to add or subtract multiple minutes.
3. Click START to start the clock.
4. Click STOP to stop the clock.

Additional Challenge(s)

Add an "alarm" feature in the program: the user should be able to set the alarm to go off at a certain time, and when that time is reached, the program should play a suitable sound.

Solutions to Feature Ideas

Feature idea # 1:

Digital clock (variables and labels):

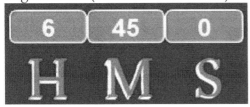

Script to set the time (owned by the "stage"):

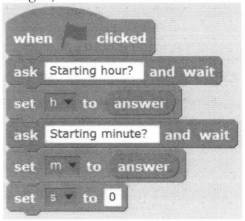

Feature idea # 2:

Step 1:

Script to draw the thick circular border:

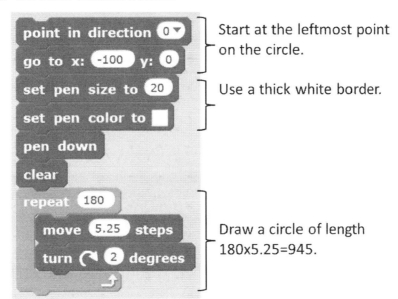

Start at the leftmost point on the circle.

Use a thick white border.

Draw a circle of length 180x5.25=945.

Step 2:

Script to draw markings for minutes:

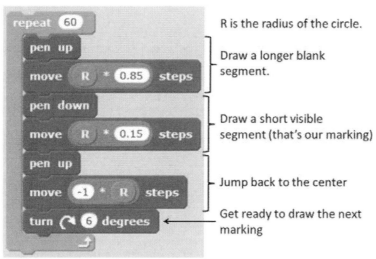

R is the radius of the circle.

Draw a longer blank segment.

Draw a short visible segment (that's our marking)

Jump back to the center

Get ready to draw the next marking

Step 3:

Script to draw hour markings:

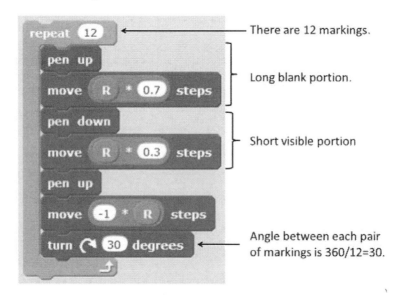

There are 12 markings.

Long blank portion.

Short visible portion

Angle between each pair of markings is 360/12=30.

Feature idea # 3:

Step 1:

Solution is given in the design itself.

Step 2:
Scripts to show time on analog clock:

Set the hour-hand:

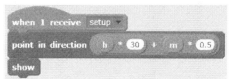

Set the minute-hand:

Feature idea # 4:

Step 1:
Script for the "second-hand":

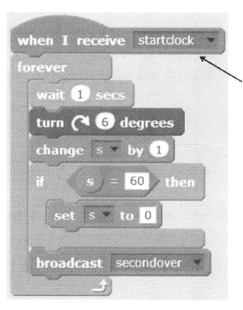

Stage will send this
Message after the clock
setup is finished.

Everything else is as per
the algorithm mentioned
above.

Step 2:
Scripts for the "minute-hand":

Message from the "second-hand" after every second:

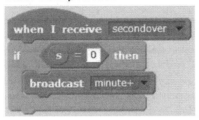

After every minute:

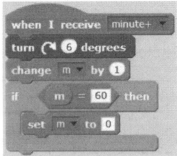

Step 3:

Scripts for the "hour-hand":

(See the algorithm above for explanation of each step)

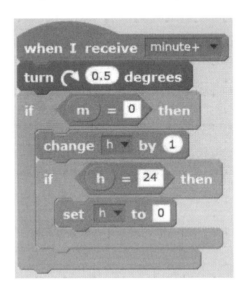

Feature idea # 5:

Step 1:

The solution is given in design itself.

Step 2:

Scripts for the start/stop button sprite:

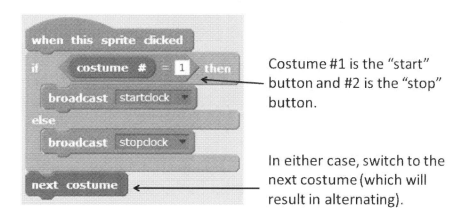

Costume #1 is the "start" button and #2 is the "stop" button.

In either case, switch to the next costume (which will result in alternating).

Step 3:
Script for the "second-hand" sprite:

Feature idea # 6:

Step 1:
Scripts for the "+" sprite:

Become visible when "set" button sends this message

Hide when clock starts running

Send message to add a minute when clicked

Step 2:
Scripts for the "−" sprite:

Become visible when "set"
button sends "modify" message:

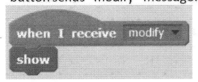

Hide when the clock starts running:

When clicked send the "minute-" message and hide:

```
when this sprite clicked
broadcast minute- ▼ and wait
```

The "modify-" script for the minute-hand:

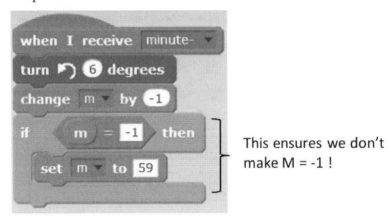

This ensures we don't
make M = -1 !

The "minute-" script for the hour-hand:

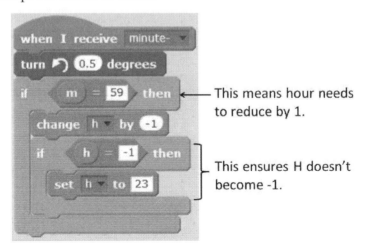

This means hour needs
to reduce by 1.

This ensures H doesn't
become -1.

Step 3:

Modified script for the "+" sprite:

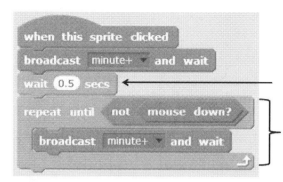

This delay ensures that a single click does not add more than a minute.

This loop will be entered only if the pointer is still pressed, and will terminate when the pointer is released.

The script for the "–" sprite would be very similar.

Phew! Setting time was a fun and challenging exercise, wasn't it?

Feature idea # 7:

Step 1:

The solution is discussed in design itself.

Step 2:

Modified script for stage (with 3 backdrops):

Initially, show the welcome screen and hide everything:

When clicked, show the next screen. If it is the final screen, do all the work as before:

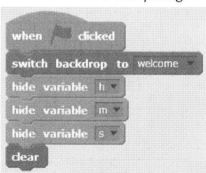

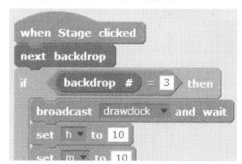

Feature idea # 8:

Script for the "CheckAMPM" procedure:

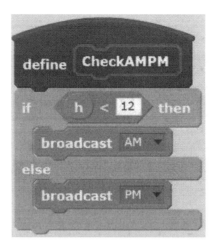

Modified "minute+" script for the "hours" sprite:

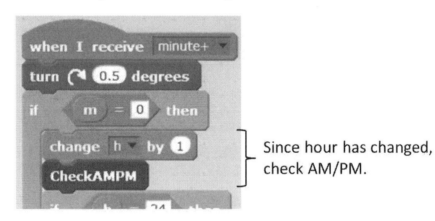

Since hour has changed, check AM/PM.

Modified "minute-" script for the "hours" sprite:

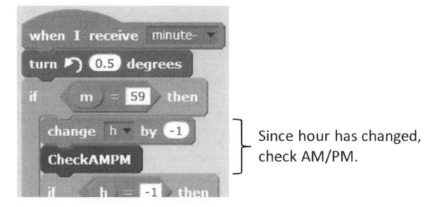

Since hour has changed, check AM/PM.

The scripts for the AM/PM sprite are quite simple:

Use the AM costume: Use the PM costume:

Feature idea # 9:

Snippet of the "minute+" script of the "hours" sprite:

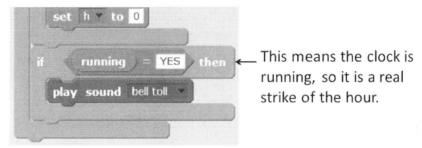

← This means the clock is running, so it is a real strike of the hour.

Modified script of the "start" button:

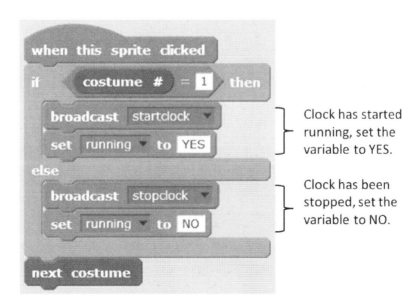

Clock has started running, set the variable to YES.

Clock has been stopped, set the variable to NO.

Feature idea # 10:

Script of one of the animation sprites: (others will have similar scripts)

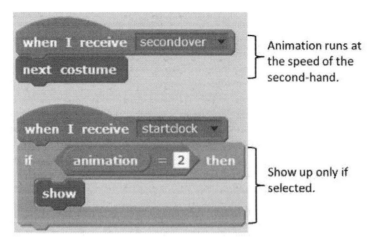

Animation runs at the speed of the second-hand.

Show up only if selected.

The "start" sprite will pick the animation:

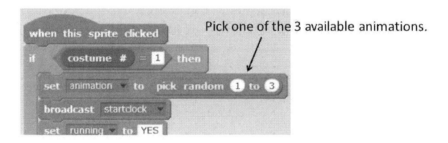

Pick one of the 3 available animations.

Programming is the only job I can think of where I get to be both an engineer and an artist. There's an incredible, rigorous, technical element to it, which I like because you have to do very precise thinking. On the other hand, it has a wildly creative side where the boundaries of imagination are the only real limitation. – Andy Hertzfeld

Project 6: Recursive Designs

Program Description

This is a program in which we will draw a few interesting "recursive" designs. A number of buttons (with names of designs as labels) are lined up along one edge of the screen. When you click any of them, a design is drawn on the screen. You can control the resulting design by entering some inputs, such as, size or angle of a shape, or the depth of recursion.

Do you want to check out a working Scratch version of this program? Click on the image below (or the URL just below it). I encourage you to explore the program and its various features. But, don't look at the Scratch scripts yet; we want to design this program ourselves!

How to run the program:

1. Click the "Green flag": everything is reset to the original state.
2. Select a design by clicking one of the buttons.
3. Enter inputs if prompted and watch the design.
4. For some of these designs (e.g. the spiral) you may want to use "Turbo mode".

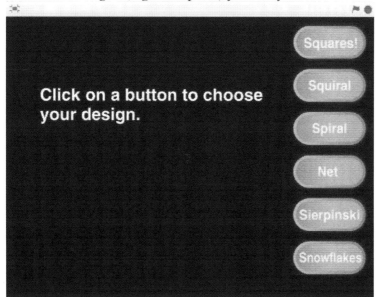

Link: https://scratch.mit.edu/projects/105188147/

Scratch and CS Concepts Used

When we design this program, we will make use of the following Scratch and CS concepts. I assume that you are already familiar with these concepts. If not, or if you want to brush up on these concepts, you should refer to the free downloadable supplement to this book at http://www.abhayjoshi.net/scratch/book1/supplement.pdf.

Main concepts:

- Algorithms
- Arithmetic operators (+, -, *, /)
- Backdrops - multiple
- Conditionals (IF and If-Else)
- Events
- Geometry - square, circle, triangle, spiral
- Logic operators (and, or, not)
- Looping - simple (repeat, forever)
- Looping - nested
- Looping - conditional (repeat until)
- Motion - absolute
- Motion - relative
- Pen commands
- Procedures
- Procedures with inputs
- Random numbers
- Recursion
- Relational operators (=, <, >)
- Scratch UI - special features
- Sequence
- Stopping scripts
- Synchronization using broadcasting
- User events (mouse)
- User input (ASK)
- User input (buttons)
- User input validation
- Variables - numbers
- Variables - properties (built-in)
- XY Geometry

High Level Design:

This is where we take a step back from the computer (literally!), analyze the problem in our mind (and on a piece of paper if necessary), and break it down into multiple smaller ideas which can be programmed separately.

Let's take a look at the various drawings created by the program and try to point out the different pieces. The program draws the following 6 types of designs:

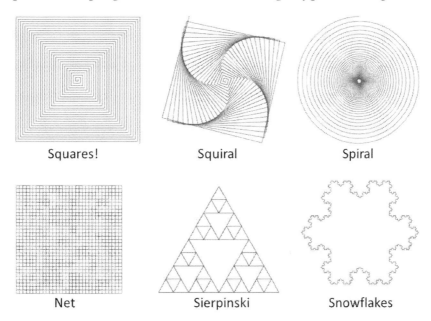

Squares!   Squiral   Spiral

Net   Sierpinski   Snowflakes

The order in which we should work on these different square designs is really up to us. We will use pencil sprites to do all the drawing. The buttons will just send messages to the pencil sprites which will then draw the appropriate design.

Does that sound like a good strategy?

Next, we will consider separately each of the six designs (Squares!, Squiral, Spiral, Net, Sierpinski, and Snowflakes) and work out how to draw it.

So, let's get rolling with these various ideas one by one. Be sure to try writing your own scripts for each idea before looking up the "Solutions" section.

Initial Set of Features:

The most important idea used in all the designs in this program is called *recursion*.

Clearly, it makes sense to start with the simplest designs and get comfortable with this idea of *recursion*. The first two designs are the simpler ones, so we will begin with those. That will be our starting version of the program. We will discuss what to do next after building this version.

For this initial version, give your project a special name (using "Save as"). For example, I am calling my copy as Recursion-1.

So, let's get rolling with these various ideas one by one.

Feature Idea # 1: Square spiral
Write a recursive procedure to draw a square spiral.

Design:
Let's first take a good look at the design itself:

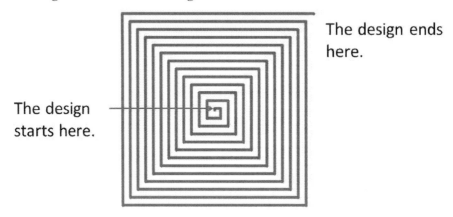

The design starts here.

The design ends here.

A recursive procedure calls itself repetitively. To draw this design recursively, we need to do the following:
- Figure out the base case (i.e. what happens in the most basic design)
- Figure out the termination condition

The basic action involves just drawing a line segment and turning right. Every recursive call draws the line a bit longer. Here is the recursive algorithm (we assume that the pen is down):

```
Procedure Foo length
     Move length
     Turn right 90
     Foo length+5
End-procedure
```

If you make this new block and call it, you will see the sprite drawing a square spiral forever!

The next task is to add a terminating condition so that the program will stop after some time. The condition basically depends on the "length" input – when it exceeds a certain value, the program should stop.

```
Procedure Foo length
If length > 200
   Return
Else
   Move length
   Turn right 90
   Foo length+5
Endif
End-procedure
```

Feature Idea # 2: Squiral
Write a recursive procedure to draw squiral designs.

Design:
Let's first take a good look at the designs for different user inputs:

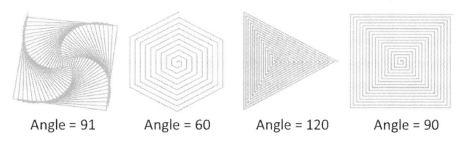

Angle = 91   Angle = 60   Angle = 120   Angle = 90

Are you surprised to see the design for angle = 90 above? Yes, it is a "square spiral" that we drew earlier! Does that give you a clue about how to draw all these designs?

Yes! Clearly, the turning angle after drawing each line segment must be responsible for these variations. Try this out to confirm our suspicion.

```
Procedure Foo length
   If length > 200
      Return
   Else
      Move length
      Turn right 91
      Foo length+5
   End-if
End-procedure
```

Different values of this angle will give us different squiral designs.

In order to get a variety of squiral designs, we should make the turning angle an input:

```
Procedure Foo length angle
   If length > 200
      Return
   Else
      Move length
      Turn right angle
      Foo length+5 angle
   End-if
End-procedure
```

The *angle* input will allow us to draw different types of squirals.

Write your own recursive procedure.

Feature Idea # 3: Combine Squares! and Squiral

Write a common recursive procedure to draw both the square spiral and squiral designs.

Design:

As we have already seen above we can use the Squiral procedure for the "square spiral" as well. Just remove the procedure for the "square spiral" and use angle=90 for the squiral, and you are done!

Feature Idea # 4: Buttons

Create button sprites for each of the designs.

Design:
We can do this easily by using broadcasting. When a button is clicked, it will send a unique broadcast message. The drawing sprite (pencil) will receive it and draw the respective design.

Save as Program Version 1
Before continuing to the next set of ideas, we will save our project. This way, we have a backup of our project that we can go back to if required for any reason.

Compare your program with my program at the link below.

Recursion-1: includes ideas 1 thru 4 explained above.
Link: https://scratch.mit.edu/projects/105188431/

How to run the program:
4. Click the "Green flag": everything is reset to the original state.
5. Select a design by clicking one of the buttons.
6. Enter inputs if prompted and watch the design.

Next Set of Features/ideas:
We will next add a real spiral and the "Net" design. The spiral is basically a circle that grows bigger and bigger with every rotation. "Net" is a mesh of horizontal and vertical wires.

For this version, make a copy of your project (using "Save as") under a different name. For example, I am calling my copy as Recursion-2.

Let's see how these designs can be drawn using recursion.

Feature Idea # 5: Curvy Spiral
Draw the curvy spiral design using recursion.

Design:
I am going to assume that you know how to draw a circle in Scratch.

It is based on the simple idea that if you move and turn continuously for a total of 360 degrees you get a circle. The following script will give you a circle:

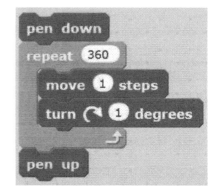

But, we want a spiral, not a circle. How do we get that? Well, a spiral, as we stated above, is a circle (or a series of circles) that grows bigger and bigger. If we draw a small portion of the circle, increase the size a bit, and then draw another small portion, increase the size again, and so on, we should get a spiral, right?

So, we will modify the above procedure to draw a quarter-circle (only 1/4th part of a full circle). We just need to change the repeat count to 90.

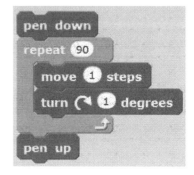

And here is the recursive algorithm to draw a spiral:

```
Procedure Spiral <len>
Repeat 90
    Move  len ←───────── The "len" input allows us to control
    Turn  right  1        the size of the circle.
End-repeat
Spiral len*1.02 ←──── Here is the recursive call. The "len"
End-procedure              input is increased just slightly. I got
                           this number 1.02 by trial and error.
```

Feature Idea # 6: Net

Draw the wire mesh "Net" design using recursion.

Design:

Let's study this design for various "depths" of recursion:

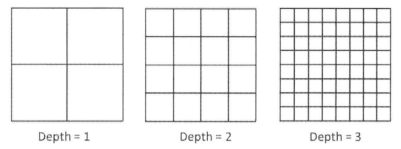

Depth = 1   Depth = 2   Depth = 3

The design itself is quite simple, and can be created using other non-recursive methods (e.g. using looping), but it would be fun to draw it using recursion.

The basic idea is to draw 4 squares in a 2x2 paned-window pattern. Using recursion, we can then go to each square and again draw the 2x2 pattern - one that fits exactly - inside it. This process can go on as deep as we wish. The program for the basic shape is shown below.

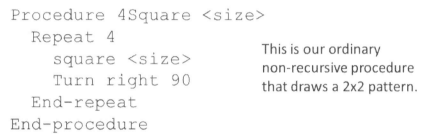

```
Procedure 4Square <size>
   Repeat 4
      square <size>
      Turn right 90
   End-repeat
End-procedure
```

This is our ordinary non-recursive procedure that draws a 2x2 pattern.

Now, in the recursive form we will jump to the center of each square and make the recursive call. The following diagram shows our approach:

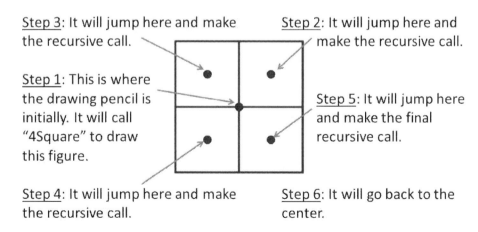

Step 3: It will jump here and make the recursive call.

Step 2: It will jump here and make the recursive call.

Step 1: This is where the drawing pencil is initially. It will call "4Square" to draw this figure.

Step 5: It will jump here and make the final recursive call.

Step 4: It will jump here and make the recursive call.

Step 6: It will go back to the center.

How do we jump to the center of each square? This is easy: we just need to move half-way vertically (along Y direction) and half-way sideways (along X direction). We will use a procedure called "Jump" for this purpose:

```
Procedure Jump <a> <b>
        Move <a>
        Turn right 90
        Move <b>
        Turn left 90
    End-procedure
```

Finally, here is the algorithm for the recursive "Net" procedure. As before, *depth* decides when to stop the recursion.

```
Procedure Net <depth> <size>
   4Square <size>
   If (depth = 1)  ←————————————  The terminating
      Stop                          condition.
   Else

                                    Jump to the center of
   Jump <size/2> <size/2>←          upper-right square.
   Repeat 4
      Net <depth-1> <size/2>←———  Recursive calls.
      Turn left 90
      Move <size>
   End-repeat                       Back to the original
   Jump <-size/2> <-size/2>←        place.
End-procedure
```

Important: Note above that after the recursive calls, the pencil sprite returns to its original position (as explained in the comments of the program).

Save as Program Version 2

Before continuing to the next set of ideas, we will save our project. This way, we have a backup of our project that we can go back to if required for any reason.

Compare your program with my program at the link below.

Recursion-2: includes ideas 5 and 6 explained above.
Link: https://scratch.mit.edu/projects/105188373/

How to run the program:
1. Click the "Green flag": everything is reset to the original state.
2. Select a design by clicking one of the buttons.
3. Enter inputs if prompted and watch the design.
4. For some of these designs (e.g. the spiral) you may want to use "Turbo mode".

Next Set of Features/ideas:
We will continue with the additional designs and add two more interesting recursive designs. One is called the "Sierpinski Triangle" named after the Polish mathematician Waclaw Sierpinski. And the other is a snowflake design.

For this version, make a copy of your project (using "Save as") under a different name. For example, I am calling my copy as Recursion-3.

Let's see how these designs can be drawn using recursion.

Feature Idea # 7: Sierpinski Triangle
Draw the Sierpinski Triangle design using recursion.

Design:
Let's take a look at the design for various values of "depth".

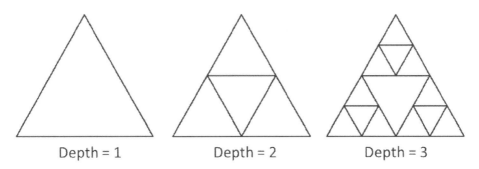

Depth = 1   Depth = 2   Depth = 3

In any graphical recursion, there is a basic shape which is redrawn during recursive calls. The recursive procedure decides where and how it is redrawn.

In this recursion:
- The basic shape is an upright (sitting) equilateral triangle,

- In every recursive call every upright triangle is filled with 3 smaller upright equilateral triangles.

First, we will design the algorithm for a utility procedure "Sitting triangle":

```
Procedure STriangle <size>
    Turn right 30
    Repeat 3
        Move <size>
        Turn right 120
    End-repeat
    Turn left 30
End-procedure
```

Now, drawing the 3 smaller triangles in a recursive manner would be straightforward as shown below.

```
Procedure Sierpinski <size> <depth>
If (depth = 1)
    STriangle <size>          ← Draw a sitting equilateral
Else                             triangle as the base case.
    Sierpinski <size/2> <depth-1>
    Turn right 90            ← This call is for the lower-
    Move <size/2>              left sub-triangle.
    Turn left 90
    Sierpinski <size/2> <depth-1>   This is for the lower-right
    Turn left 30            ← sub-triangle.
    Move <size/2>
    Turn right 30
    Sierpinski <size/2> <depth-1>← This is for the upper
    Turn left 150              sub-triangle.
    Move <size/2>
    Turn right 150          ←Return back to the
End-if                        starting point.
End- procedure
```

Optional challenge: Instead of drawing 3 sub-triangles it would be more efficient (faster) to simply draw the central upside-down triangle by connecting the mid-points of each edge. Try this yourself.

Feature Idea # 8: Snowflakes

Draw the snowflakes design using recursion.

Design:

Let's take a look at the design for various values of "depth".

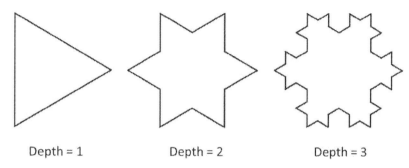

Depth = 1   Depth = 2   Depth = 3

If you see carefully, the basic shape is a wrinkly edge (a line segment that is pulled up at the center). We start with an equilateral triangle, and then in subsequent recursive calls every straight edge is replaced by this wrinkly edge. If we can figure out the wrinkle pattern for a single line, that same pattern is repeated 3 times for the triangle. So, we will first write a recursive procedure for one edge of the triangle.

If you inspect carefully, the wrinkly edge is created when the middle 1/3rd portion of the straight line segment is pulled up into a spike.

So, here is our recursive procedure for a single line segment:

```
Procedure FlakeLine <length> <depth>
  If <depth> = 1                              The base case is just
    Pen down                                  drawing a straight
    Move <length>                             line.
    Pen up
  Else                                        At every recursive
    FlakeLine <length>/3 <depth-1>            step, the line gets
    Turn left 60                              divided into 4 equal
    FlakeLine <length>/3 <depth-1>            line segments.
    Turn right 120
    FlakeLine <length>/3 <depth-1>
    Turn left 60
    FlakeLine <length>/3 <depth-1>
  End-if
End-procedure
```

And now, the triangle itself which is our snowflake:

```
Procedure snowflake <size> <depth>
    Repeat 3
        FlakeLine <size> <depth>
        Turn right 120
    End-repeat
End-procedure
```

Save as Program Version 3

Before continuing to the next set of ideas, we will save our project. This way, we have a backup of our project that we can go back to if required for any reason.

Compare your program with my program at the link below.

Recursion-3: includes ideas 7 and 8 explained above.
Link: https://scratch.mit.edu/projects/105188244/

How to run the program:
1. Click the "Green flag": everything is reset to the original state.
2. Select a design by clicking one of the buttons.
3. Enter inputs if prompted and watch the design.
4. For some of these designs (e.g. the spiral) you may want to use "Turbo mode".

Final Set of Features/ideas:

We have finished all designs that we had planned. But, there are a few enhancements that will make this program more robust and user-friendly. For example, there is no validation of user input – to check whether it is in the expected range. We will add this validation check. Secondly, some of our designs grow continuously and can get distorted when the drawing sprite goes near the screen edges. We will figure out a general solution to this problem. Finally, we can use our snowflake design to paint the sky (i.e. our screen) with lots of snowflakes – big and small, with all sorts of colors – you get the idea!

For this final version, make a copy of your project (using "Save as") under a different name. For example, I am calling my copy as Recursion-final.

So, let's get cracking with these ideas!

Feature Idea # 9: User input validation

Right now, whenever we ask the user to enter some number input, we don't validate if it is in an expected range. Add this validation check.

Design:

Basically, we want to ensure that the user input is within an expected range.

For example, in the "Net" design, we ask the user to enter the depth of the recursion. This can't be less than 1. It also cannot be too large. In fact, after a certain depth, the drawing becomes indistinguishable, and the program takes a very long time to finish. So, we would like to put an upper limit also.

How do we ensure the user does not exceed these limits?

What we can do is, check the input and ask again and again until the input is valid.

Here is how the algorithm would look:

```
Procedure UserInput <lower> <upper>
    Ask user for input.
    N = input
    Repeat until N>lower and N<upper
        Ask user for input.
        N = input
    End-repeat
End-procedure
```

Feature Idea # 10: Prevent screen overflow

Some of the recursive designs grow continuously and thus can exceed the screen size. Right now, we have put limits within the recursive procedures to prevent this. Figure out a general solution such that any drawing will automatically stop as soon as the drawing sprite touches any of the screen edges.

Design:

We know the screen dimensions in Scratch: the X axis goes from -240 to +240 and the Y axis goes from -180 to +180. We wish to design a mechanism such that the drawing never goes out of these ranges.

How can we achieve this?

Well, if you think about it, we need a way in which we can *sense* whenever the X or Y position of the drawing sprite goes out of range. If we can do that, we can immediately stop the drawing scripts.

So, how do we continuously sense the X and Y positions of a sprite?

We can use the built-in Scratch variables "x position" and "y position" and compare them with the upper and lower limits as given above. As soon as any of the limits is crossed, we can stop the scripts.

Feature Idea # 11: Snowfall!

Use the snowflake design to paint the sky (i.e. our screen) with lots of snowflakes – with different sizes and colors.

Design:

We already have a procedure that draws a snowflake. Now, we just need to draw a bunch of them on the screen. We can use the random operator to jump to random locations on the screen, use random colors, and use random sizes for each snowflake.

Do you get the idea?

But, when do we draw this "snowfall"? There is no separate button for this. Well, we could simply ask the user. Before asking for the snowflake's depth of recursion, we will ask the user to enter "1" for a single flake, or "2" for snowfall.

Save as Program Final Version

Congratulations! You have completed all the main features of the program. As before, let's save this project.

Compare your program with my program at the link below.

Recursion-final: includes ideas 9 thru 11 explained above.
Link: https://scratch.mit.edu/projects/105188147/

How to run the program:
1. Click the "Green flag": everything is reset to the original state.
2. Select a design by clicking on one of the buttons.
3. Enter inputs if prompted and watch the design.
4. For some of these designs (e.g. the spiral) you may want to use "Turbo mode".

Solutions to Feature Ideas

Feature idea # 1:
Here is the recursive procedure:

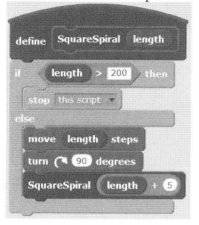

Feature idea # 2:
Here is the recursive procedure:

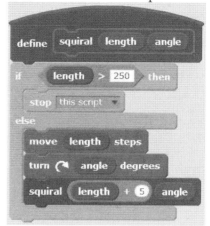

Feature idea # 4:
For example, the following script is for the "squiral" button:

This message is for all buttons to hide so that the screen is cleared.

This message is for the pencil to draw the design.

And this is a part of the "receiving" script for the drawing sprite (pencil):

We will have similar broadcasting connections for the other buttons.

Feature idea # 5:

Script for the pencil sprite to draw a spiral:

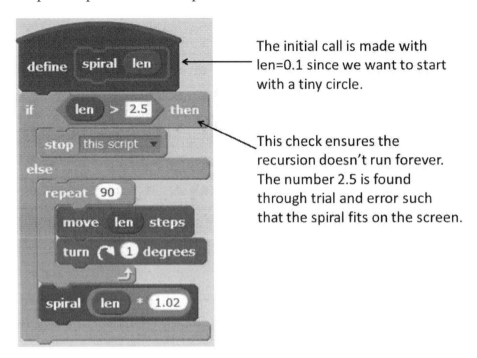

The initial call is made with len=0.1 since we want to start with a tiny circle.

This check ensures the recursion doesn't run forever. The number 2.5 is found through trial and error such that the spiral fits on the screen.

Feature idea # 6:

Pencil script for drawing the "Net" design:

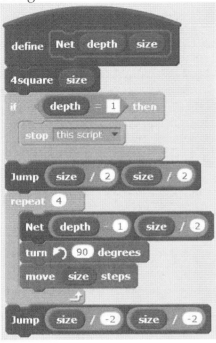

Feature idea # 7:

Pencil script for drawing Sierpinski design:

Feature idea # 9:

You will have to copy this script for every pencil sprite if applicable:

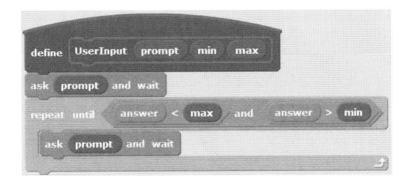

And here is a sample call to this procedure from the "Net" design:

We wish to allow the recursion level to be anywhere from 1 to 6.

```
clear
UserInput  Enter depth level: (>0 and <7)  0  7
Net  answer  140
```

Feature idea # 8:

Pencil script for the FlakeLine procedure:

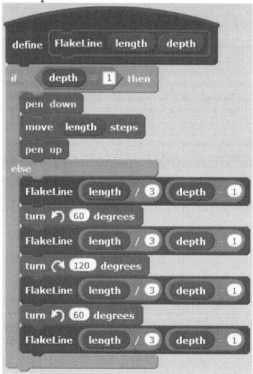

```
define  FlakeLine  length  depth

if    depth  =  1  then
    pen down
    move  length  steps
    pen up
else
    FlakeLine  length / 3  depth - 1
    turn ↺ 60 degrees
    FlakeLine  length / 3  depth - 1
    turn ↻ 120 degrees
    FlakeLine  length / 3  depth - 1
    turn ↺ 60 degrees
    FlakeLine  length / 3  depth - 1
```

Feature idea # 10:

The pencil sprite will use this script to start sensing if the drawing is getting too close to the screen edges. The actual drawing script should start this sensing script.

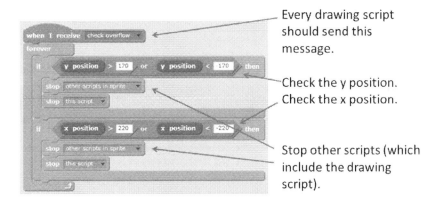

Every drawing script should send this message.

Check the y position.
Check the x position.

Stop other scripts (which include the drawing script).

Feature idea # 11:

Pencil script that asks user what to draw:

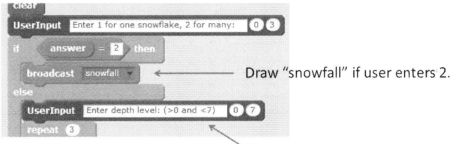

Draw "snowfall" if user enters 2.

Else proceed to draw a single snowflake.

Pencil script that draws "snowfall":

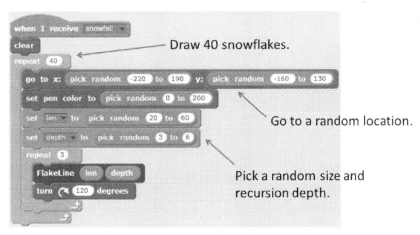

Draw 40 snowflakes.

Go to a random location.

Pick a random size and recursion depth.

The computer programmer ... is a creator of universes for which he alone is the lawgiver ... universes of virtually unlimited complexity can be created in the form of computer programs. Moreover ... systems so formulated and elaborated act out their programmed scripts. They compliantly obey their laws and vividly exhibit their obedient behavior. No playwright, no stage director, no emperor, however powerful, has ever exercised such absolute authority to arrange a stage or a field of battle and to command such unswervingly dutiful actors or troops.

- Joseph Weizenbaum

Project 7: Picture Cards

Program Description

This is a game you play with a bunch of picture cards. You have several pairs of identical cards placed face down on the screen. You click on any two cards; if they match, you get points and the two cards disappear. If they don't match, they turn face down again. By remembering the cards you try to click on matching cards in future rounds.

Do you want to check out a working Scratch version of this program? Click on the image below (or the URL just below it). I encourage you to explore the program and its various features. But, don't look at the Scratch scripts yet; we want to design this program ourselves!

How to run the program:
1. Click the "Green flag": the cards will be placed randomly on the screen.
2. Re-arrange the cards with your mouse if you want, but don't click.
3. Click the cards to start playing the game.

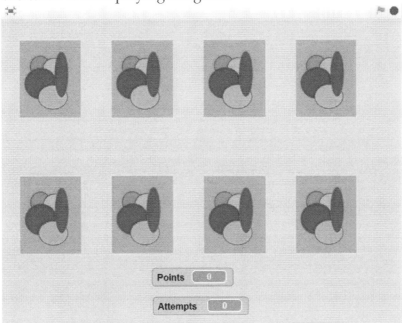

Link: https://scratch.mit.edu/projects/106144703/

Scratch and CS Concepts Used

When we design this program, we will make use of the following Scratch and CS concepts. I assume that you are already familiar with these concepts. If not, or if you want to brush up on these concepts, you should refer to the free downloadable supplement to this book at http://www.abhayjoshi.net/scratch/book1/supplement.pdf.

Main concepts:
- Algorithms
- Conditionals (If-Else)
- Conditionals (IF)
- Conditionals (Wait until)
- Conditionals (nested IF)
- Costumes
- Events
- Looping - simple (repeat, forever)
- Motion - absolute
- Random numbers
- Relational operators (=, <, >)
- Sounds - playing sounds
- Synchronization using broadcasting
- User events (mouse)
- User input (buttons)
- Variables - numbers
- Variables - strings
- XY Geometry

Additional concepts (for the advanced versions):
- Arithmetic operators (+, -, *, /)
- Arithmetic expressions
- Looping - nested
- OOP - creating instances using clones
- Variables – lists
- Variables - properties (built-in)
- Variables - local/global scope

High Level Design:

This is where we take a step back from the computer (literally!), analyze the problem in our mind (and on a piece of paper if necessary), and break it down into multiple smaller ideas which can be programmed separately.

We will first consider a very basic version of the game in which there are only 2 pairs of picture cards: say, two *cats* and two *butterflies*.

Obviously, we will need one sprite for each card. So, for 2 pairs of cards we will need 4 sprites. Each sprite will have 2 costumes: the picture (such as "cat") and the backside (which would be the same for all cards).

Next, we can consider this game to be played in a series of "sessions", where each session consists of picking two cards. If the cards match, the player gets a point, else, the cards turn face down again.

So, one way to design this program is to first work out this idea of a "session".

Initial Version

Implement the idea of a session in which two cards are picked and compared.

For this initial version, give your project a special name (using "Save as"). For example, I am calling my copy as Picturecards-1.

Feature Idea # 1: Session

Implement the idea of a session in which two cards are picked and compared.

Design:

Picking a card would be the same as clicking a card. To count the number of cards clicked, we will use a variable called *numclicks*.

How will you compare the two clicked cards?

To compare, we could use two more variables, say *card1* and *card2*, which will hold the "names" of the picked cards. Obviously, each pair of cards will need to have a unique name, such as "*cat*" or "*butterfly*". When a card sprite is clicked, it will save its name in one of these variables (*card1* or *card2*). The job of comparing cards can then be done by a separate sprite or the stage.

How will a card know where to store its name when it is clicked? In *card1* or *card2*? The card cannot possibly know whether it's the first one to be clicked or the second one.

Well, we can have it simply check which one of the two variables is still empty (or 0) and use that one to store its name! That should solve that problem.

Here is the algorithm for this idea:

```
When the card is clicked:
Turn face up
Set variable face = up
If card1=0
   Set card1 = name          This variable is
Else                          explained later below
   Set card2 = name
Endif
Add 1 to numclicks
```

We will have the stage perform the card comparison; but, how will it know when two cards have been clicked?

It can find out by continuously monitoring the value of the variable *numclicks*.

After the comparison, if the cards match, stage will send a message to the cards to "hide". To ensure only the cards facing up hide, each card will have its own private variable called *face* which will have the value "down" if the card is facing down, and "up" if the card is facing up.

The stage will then send a "new session" message to begin a new card-picking session.

See the stage algorithm below.

```
Forever:
Send "new session"                      Start a new session.
Set variable numclicks = 0
Wait until numclicks = 2                 Session ends after
If card1 = card2                         2 clicks.
   Send "hide cards"          Compare cards.
Endif
```

What should each card do upon receiving the "hide cards" signal? This signal is only meant for the cards that are facing up.

```
When "hide cards" received
If face = up
   Hide
Endif
```

And what should each card do upon receiving the "new session" signal? It should just turn face down to get ready for the next session.

```
When "new session" received
Turn face down
Set face = down
```

What should the stage do upon receiving the "new session" signal? It should initialize these global variables to 0 to get ready for the next card picking session:

```
Set card1 = card2 = 0
```

All these ideas should give us a basic working version of the game.

Save as Program Version 1

Before continuing to the next set of ideas, we will save our project. This way, we have a backup of our project that we can go back to if required for any reason.

Compare your program with my program at the link below.

Picturecards-1: includes idea 1 explained above.
Link: https://scratch.mit.edu/projects/106144592/

How to run the program:
1. Click the "Green flag": the cards will be placed on the screen.
2. Click the cards to start playing the game.

Next Set of Features/ideas:

Count the points earned by the player, i.e. the number of times the two picked cards match.

In our previous version, the cards appear at the exact same places on the screen. This, of course, is a problem, because, the player already knows which card is where! Make the cards appear at different places every time the game is started.

While we are at it, add a few more picture cards to make the game more interesting.

For this version, make a copy of your project (using "Save as") under a different name. For example, I am calling my copy as Picturecards-2.

Feature Idea # 2: Count points

Count the points earned by the player, i.e. the number of times the two picked cards match.

Design:

We will add a variable called *Points* to count points. We need to modify the stage scripts to do two things: (1) Initialize *Points* to 0 at the very beginning, and (2) Increment it by 1 when there is a match.

Feature Idea # 3: Card placement

In our previous version, the cards appear at the exact same places on the screen. This, of course, is a problem, because, the player already knows which card is where! Make the cards appear at different places every time the game is started.

Design:

Basically, we want the cards to appear at different places every time we start the program. We could use the *Random* operator to place each card at a random place on the screen. It will be like shuffling a pack of cards and throwing them in the game area.

The player can then manually drag the cards with the pointer and rearrange them so that they don't overlap each other. Normally, Scratch doesn't allow users to drag sprites in the full-screen mode. To change that setting, click on the "i" symbol of each sprite (as shown below) and then check the box "can drag in player".

Feature Idea # 4: More cards

While we are at it, add a few more picture cards to make the game more interesting.

Design:

This is easy: add new picture sprites such that each sprite has two costumes: the picture itself and the back side (identical to other sprites). The back side costume must have the name *costume1*. The scripts would be mostly identical.

The program at the link below now has 8 cards (or 4 pairs of picture cards).

Save as Program Version 2

Before continuing to the next set of ideas, we will save our project. This way, we have a backup of our project that we can go back to if required for any reason.

Compare your program with my program at the link below.

Picturecards-2: includes ideas 2, 3, and 4 explained above.
Link: https://scratch.mit.edu/projects/106144647/

How to run the program:
1. Click the "Green flag": the cards will be placed randomly on the screen.
2. Re-arrange the cards with your mouse if you want, but don't click.
3. Click the cards to start playing the game.

Final Set of Features/ideas:
You might have noticed that our current program has a bug: it allows the player to click the same card twice and win points. Fix this problem.

When we insert additional picture sprites in our program, we have to resize all picture cards to ensure they fit on the screen. It is tedious and error-prone to resize every card manually. Fix this problem.

Similar to counting "points", we should also count the number of attempts.

Use sound clips to make the game more fun to play.

For this final version, make a copy of your project (using "Save as") under a different name. For example, I am calling my copy as Picturecards-final.

Feature Idea # 5: Click only once
Our current program allows the player to click on the same card twice and win points. Fix this problem.

Design:
Basically, when a card is clicked it should react only if it is closed (i.e. has its face down). We just need to add this check in the script.

Feature Idea # 6: Fit cards to the screen
When we insert additional picture sprites in our program, we have to resize all picture cards to ensure they fit on the screen. It is tedious and error-prone to resize every card manually. Fix this problem.

Design:

We can use the "set size" command in the setup script of each card. For example, the command below will set the size to 70% of the sprite's original size.

There is still a small inconvenience. If we decide to change the number to say 50, we have to go to each card and change this number in its script.

To get rid of this inconvenience, we can use a variable called *cardsize* as a remote control! That way, we can simply change the value of the variable *cardsize* and all cards will automatically change to that size.

Modify your own script.

Feature Idea # 7: Count attempts

Similar to counting "points", we should also count the number of attempts.

Design:

This is quite straightforward. We will employ another variable called *"attempts"*. This variable will be incremented every time the player clicks a pair of cards – whether they match or not.

Feature Idea # 8: Sounds

Use sound bites to make the game more fun to play.

Design:

This is quite straightforward. At every card click we will play a sound clip, and also when the cards match. Use whatever sounds you like.

Save as Final Program Version

Congratulations, this is our final program! Save it as picturecards-final.sb2.

Compare your program with my program at the link below.

Picturecards-final: includes ideas 5, 6, 7, and 8 explained above.
Link: https://scratch.mit.edu/projects/106144703/

How to run the program:

1. Click the "Green flag": the cards will be placed randomly on the screen.
2. Re-arrange the cards with your mouse if you want, but don't click.
3. Click the cards to start playing the game.

Advanced Features

We have a working version of the game. But, there are a few more interesting features that we can add to make it efficient and versatile.

For example, managing each card as a separate sprite is tedious: any change we make to one card (appearance or scripts) must be duplicated to all other cards manually. Instead, if we figure out how to use a single sprite and the idea of clones, this headache will go away.

In the current version, the set of pictures is the same every time we play the game. It would be nice to select cards from a large bank of pictures. Consider using clones to implement this feature.

For this advanced version, make a copy of your project (using "Save as") under a different name. For example, I am calling my copy as Picturecards-adv-1.

Feature Idea # 9: Clones

Right now, adding a new picture card requires inserting a pair of sprites and copying all the scripts. The number of sprites can get out of hand in this approach. Consider using clones to simplify this task.

Design:

Let us consider using a single main sprite such that:

- The first costume is the "backside" of each picture card
- Subsequent costumes are all possible picture cards (e.g. cat, dinosaur, butterfly, frog, etc.) with the appropriate costume names

See the picture below to get an idea of what we are proposing:

From our experience so far with this game, we know that each picture card visible on the screen needs the following things:

1. A variable that contains its name (e.g. "cat" or "dinosaur" etc.)
2. A variable that contains its state (face "up" or "down")
3. The ability to switch between the "picture" and the "backside" of the card

Let's see if a clone of the main sprite (as described above) will meet these requirements in order to work as a picture card on the screen.

From the "clones" concept we know that each clone gets its own copy of the sprite's private variables. So if the main sprite has private variables called "face" and "name", each clone will get its own separate copy of these variables. We can use the following Scratch properties (built-in variables) to get the costume # and the costume name.

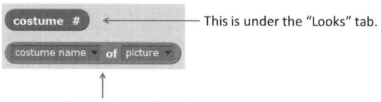

This is under the "Looks" tab.

This is under the "Sensing" tab.

So, points 1 and 2 above are addressed.

Next, the clone needs access to the costumes of the "backside" and its own picture to address point 3 above. Each clone, immediately after starting, can save its costume number in a private variable. That way, it can switch to that costume (using the "switch to costume" command) any time.

So, we seem to be all set to use clones!

Rest of the scripts will remain more or less the same. You may want to consider adding a "Start game" button so that "Green flag" will set things up for the game, and "Start game" will actually start the game.

Feature Idea # 10: Bank of cards

In the current version, the set of pictures is the same every time we play the game. It would be nice to select cards from a large bank of pictures. Consider using clones to implement this feature.

Design:

If you think about this for a minute, it is not very hard at all. Since we are now using costumes for the pictures, we can simply load up as many costumes as we want in the main sprite. Then, we can randomly select any 4 and use them for the game. That way, the player will see different cards every time.

But, how do we pick 4 costumes randomly and pass them on to the clones?

Right now, we start from the 2nd costume and take the next 4 costumes. Think about this as a "window". If we simply slide this window to a different starting costume, we will have a different set of 4 costumes. Got it?

Save as Program Advanced Version 1

Before continuing to the next set of ideas, we will save our project. This way, we have a backup of our project that we can go back to if required for any reason.

Compare your program with my program at the link below.

Picturecards-adv-1: includes ideas 9 and 10 explained above.
Link: https://scratch.mit.edu/projects/106144763/

How to run the program:
1. Click the "Green flag": things will be set up for the game.
2. Click "Start game" to start the game. Cards will appear at random places.
3. Re-arrange the cards with your mouse if you want, but don't click.
4. Click the cards to start playing the game.

Feature Idea # 11: Automatic placement

The player has to manually arrange the picture cards on the screen. Can you automate this step?

(For this advanced version, make a copy of your project (using "Save as") under a different name. For example, I am calling my copy as Picturecards-adv-2.)

Design:

Let's see. We want to arrange 8 cards in 2 neat rows of 4 cards each. The arrangement essentially looks like a table of 2 rows and 4 columns, right? We will call each location in this table as a "cell". These cells can be numbered 1 to 8 as shown below:

1	2	3	4
5	6	7	8

To place a card in a cell, we could just use the "Go to x, y" command if we knew the X and Y co-ordinates of the cell (i.e. of its center).

Each picture card (i.e. its respective clone) can be assigned an id 1 thru 8 based on the sequence of its birth. We will use a local variable called *myid* for this purpose. If you remember, each clone gets its own copy of this variable.

So far, so good! Now, we just need someone to assign these cells one by one to a randomly selected clone. How do we do that?

Here is the overall algorithm:
1. Create a list L of numbers 1 to 8 (since we have 8 cards).
2. Shuffle numbers 1 to 8 in the list L. We will use Donald Knuth's standard algorithm for this purpose. (See https://scratch.mit.edu/projects/65352234/ for a demo of this algorithm)
3. For each number in this list:
    a. Save it in a global variable (say *cell_id*).
    b. Find the X and Y coordinates of the next available cell and save them in global variables "x" and "y".
    c. Send a message "place" to all clones. Only the clone whose id matches *cell_id* will respond to this message.

How will you do step 3b? That is, how will you calculate the x and y of the center of each cell in the 2x2 table shown above?

Here is the algorithm for this calculation:

```
Set variables startx, starty (center of cell
    row 1, column 1)
Set variables height, width (of each cell;
    same for all)
Set rows=2, columns=4
Repeat 2
  Row = 0, 1
  Repeat 4
    Column = 0, 1, 2, 3
    X = startx + Column * width
    Y = starty - Row * height
  End-repeat
End-repeat
```

Algorithm for the clone script:

```
When I receive message "place"
If cell_id = myid
  Go to x, y
Endif
```

Save as Program Advanced Version 2

Congratulations! This is our final advanced version.

Compare your program with my program at the link below.

Picturecards-adv-2: includes idea 11 explained above.
Link: https://scratch.mit.edu/projects/106144808/

How to run the program:
1. Click the "Green flag": things will be set up for the game.
2. Click "Start game" to start the game. Cards will be arranged automatically.
3. Click the cards to start playing the game.

Solutions to Feature Ideas

Feature idea # 2:

The modified scripts are shown below:

Initialize points to 0.   Increment it by 1 if the cards match.

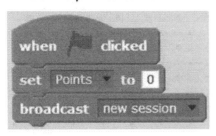
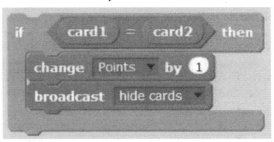

Feature idea # 3:

The following command will place each card at a new location when you restart the game:

The following picture shows how to allow the user to move sprites in the full-screen mode:

This checkbox decides whether the sprite can be moved in full-screen mode.

Feature idea # 5:

The following snippet shows the modification to the script.

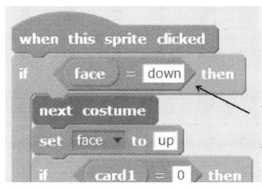

This check ensures that the card click works only when the card is facing down.

Feature idea # 6:

See the modified script below.

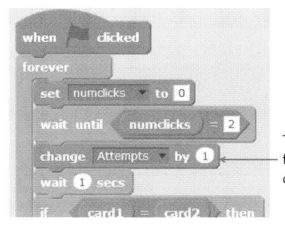

Feature idea # 7:

See the modified stage script below.

The variable is incremented for every session of card clicks.

Feature idea # 8:

The following script snippets show where to insert the sounds.

Stage script:

Card script:

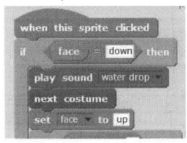

Feature idea # 9:

The parent (i.e. the main sprite) will run the following script to create clones:

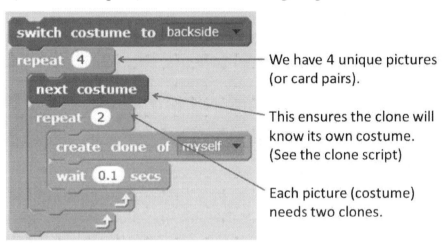

We have 4 unique pictures (or card pairs).

This ensures the clone will know its own costume. (See the clone script)

Each picture (costume) needs two clones.

Clone script (when it starts as a clone):

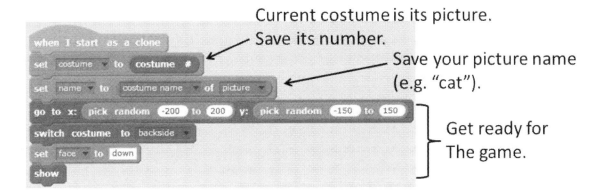

Current costume is its picture.
Save its number.

Save your picture name
(e.g. "cat").

Get ready for
The game.

Feature idea # 10:

This script moves the "window" to a random starting point in a list of 22 costumes.

1st costume is the common "backside".

This takes us to a costume from 1st thru 18th, so that the next 4 costumes are picture costumes.

The best programmers are not marginally better than merely good ones. They are an order-of-magnitude better, measured by whatever standard: conceptual creativity, speed, ingenuity of design, or problem-solving ability.
– Randall E. Stross

Program Description

The Tower of Hanoi is a mathematical game or puzzle. It consists of three rods, and a number of discs of different sizes which can slide onto any rod. The puzzle starts with the discs in a neat stack in ascending order of size on one rod, the smallest at the top, thus making a conical shape. See the picture below (Courtesy Wikipedia).

The objective of the puzzle is to move the entire stack to another rod, while obeying the following simple rules:

1. Only one disc can be moved at a time.
2. A disk can be moved only if it is the uppermost disc on a stack.
3. You cannot place a bigger disc on top of a smaller disc.

With three discs, the puzzle can be solved in seven moves.

Do you want to check out a working Scratch version of this program? Click on the image below (or the URL just below it). I encourage you to explore the program and its various features. But, don't look at the Scratch scripts yet; we want to design this program ourselves!

How to run the program:

1. Click the "Green flag": a help screen appears. Read the instructions carefully.
2. Click anywhere to continue.
3. Using the "Discs" slider pick the number of discs: 1 to 5.
4. Click "Setup" to arrange the discs on one of the rods.
5. Press SPACEBAR to move the discs yourself, one disc at a time.

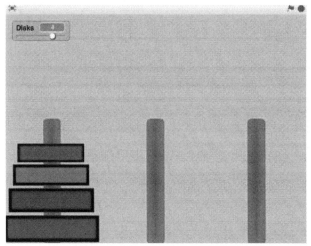

Link: https://scratch.mit.edu/projects/87006602/

Scratch and CS Concepts Used

When we design this program, we will make use of the following Scratch and CS concepts. I assume that you are already familiar with these concepts. If not, or if you want to brush up on these concepts, you should refer to the free downloadable supplement to this book at http://www.abhayjoshi.net/scratch/book1/supplement.pdf.

Main concepts:

- Algorithms
- Arithmetic operators (+, -, *, /)
- Arithmetic expressions
- Arithmetic operators (mod, floor, etc.)
- Conditionals (If-Else)
- Conditionals (IF)
- Conditionals (nested IF)
- Costumes
- Events
- Events - coordinating multiple user events
- Logic operators (and, or, not)
- Looping - simple (repeat, forever)
- Looping - conditional (repeat until)
- Motion - absolute
- Procedures
- Relational operators (=, <, >)

- Sensing touch
- Sequence
- Sounds - playing sounds
- String operations (join, letter, length of)
- Synchronization using broadcasting
- User events (mouse)
- User input (buttons)
- Variables - numbers
- Variables - strings
- Variables - properties (built-in)
- Variables - as counters
- Variables - as gates
- Variables - as remote control
- XY Geometry

Additional concepts (for the advanced version):
- Procedures with inputs
- Recursion

High Level Design:

This is where we take a step back from the computer (literally!), analyze the problem in our mind (and on a piece of paper if necessary), and break it down into multiple smaller ideas which can be programmed separately.

Let's take a look at the main screen of the game and try to point out the different pieces.

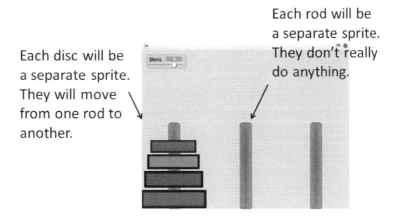

Each disc will be a separate sprite. They will move from one rod to another.

Each rod will be a separate sprite. They don't really do anything.

Initial Set of Features:

Clearly it makes sense to start with the most basic apparatus – which is the 3 rods and 3 discs. At this stage, we *won't* trouble ourselves with the rules of the game (as listed in "program description" above), specifically #2 and #3. We will implement the basic feature of moving a disc from one rod to another. How will the program know which disc is to be moved and to which rod? Well, we will ask the user to click on a rod to set "destination" and then click on any disc to move it to that rod. Finally we will add a help screen.

That will be our starting version of the game. We will discuss what to do next after building this version.

For this initial version, give your project a special name (using "Save as"). For example, I am calling my copy as Hanoi-1.

So, let's get rolling with these various ideas one by one.

Feature Idea # 1: The Rods and the Discs
Draw the rod sprites and the disc sprites.

Design:
I think this is so easy you won't need any help. But, just consider the following guidelines:
- The rods are identical, so, draw one and replicate the others.
- Position the rods such that they are spaced out properly.
- The discs have decreasing (or increasing) sizes.
- When a disc is moved it will need to be aware of other discs, by *sensing touch*. So, use a thick border for each disc to allow this sensing. Use the same border color for all.
- You could in fact draw just one disc and replicate it (and then resize and change its inside color).

Feature Idea # 2: Disc movements
When the user clicks on a disc, it should slide out of its rod and slide into the destination rod.

Step 1: When clicked, slide the disc upwards until it is out of its rod.

Design:

In order to move only vertically, each disc should only change its Y coordinate. Since each rod is of identical height, we only need to move each disc to a fixed height. To get smooth motion, we could use the "glide" command.

Step 2: Move the disc just above the "destination" rod.

Design:

This task involves two problems. One is figuring out the "destination" rod. We can solve this problem by having a variable *dest* (or *destination* if you prefer) which will tell the disc the sprite name of the target rod. This variable will be set every time the user clicks on a rod.

The second problem is moving the disc to the destination rod, which is a simple matter of gliding to a point horizontally just above the target rod. We can use the "x position of" property (built-in variable) to find out the X position of the target rod.

Step 3: Drop the disc in the "destination" rod.

Design:

This task basically involves gliding the disc down on the destination rod until it reaches the bottom or another disc which might already be there. We can use the "Repeat until" command to lower the disc until one of these conditions becomes true. Sensing the bottom is easy: we can compare the disc's "y position" with the y position of the bottom of the rod. Sensing the top disc which might be there already is also not so difficult: we can use the "touching color" condition.

Feature Idea # 3: Help screen

Add a help screen before starting the game, telling the player how to move the discs.

Design:

This should be straightforward. You can check out the scripts in the program below.

Save as Program Version 1

Before continuing to the next set of ideas, we will save our project. This way, we have a backup of our project that we can go back to if required for any reason.

Compare your program with my program at the link below.
Hanoi-1: includes ideas 1 thru 3 explained above.
Link: https://scratch.mit.edu/projects/87138145/

How to run the program:
1. Click the "Green flag": a help screen appears. Read the instructions carefully.
2. Click anywhere to start the game.
3. Click a rod to choose "destination" and then click any disc to move it to that rod.

Next Set of Features/ideas:
We will continue with 3 discs. Next, we will try to enforce rule #2 of the game, that is, only the top disc in a rod will be allowed to move. Therefore, instead of clicking on a disc to initiate a move, we will ask the user to (1) press SPACE BAR to initiate a move, and (2) click on two rods: "source" and "destination". The top disc (if any) in the "source" rod will then move to the top of the "destination" rod. We may still violate rule #3 of the game, but about that we will worry later. We should also ensure that when the game begins, all the discs are stacked up properly on the left-most rod.

For this version, make a copy of your project (using "Save as") under a different name. For example, I am calling my copy as Hanoi-2.

Let us get cracking with these ideas and features one by one.

Feature Idea # 4: Track discs of each rod
If you think about the changes we want to make in this version, we will first need to figure out a way in which each rod will know about its own stack of discs. For example, initially when the game begins, all the discs 1, 2, and 3 (in that order) will be with rod T1. If the user moves disc 3 to rod T3, T1 will be left with discs 1 & 2 and T3 will have disc 3.

Design:
The best way to store information is to use variables. We will need to have a separate variable for each rod. Let's call them L1, L2, and L3. These variables will tell which discs are currently mounted on each rod.

So, initially, when the game begins, L1 will contain "123" because T1 has all the discs, and L2 and L3 will be blank (empty) because there are no discs on T2 and T3.

If the user moves disc 3 to rod T3, L1 will change to "12", L3 will become "3", and L2 will remain blank.

Do you get the idea?

So, for this particular feature, we just need to define a separate local variable for each rod, and initialize it appropriately when the game begins. How these variables will actually change during the course of the game, we will consider later as we add more related features.

Feature Idea # 5: Source and destination rods

To move a disc, the program needs to know the source rod (where to move from) and the destination rod (where to move to). Ask user to click and specify.

Design:

This is a slightly tricky feature to program. When the user clicks on a rod, the rod has no way to know whether it is the "source" or the "destination". It all depends on which rod was clicked first, right?

There are many different ways in which we can program this. For example, we could have a variable which would tell which rod was clicked first.

I am going to suggest a different approach.

It seems clear to me that we will need to *prompt* the user that he/she should click on a rod to pick the source, and then click on another rod to pick the destination. We will make use of this very need *to prompt the user* to solve our problem above.

We will use a separate sprite called "prompt" that will display these prompts by changing costumes. First, when a disc move is requested (by pressing SPACE BAR), this sprite will show the prompt *Click on the source rod*. As soon as the user clicks on a rod, that rod's name will be saved in a global variable called *source*. The "prompt" sprite will then change its costume that says *Click on the destination rod*. As soon as the user clicks on a second rod, that rod's name will be saved in another global variable called *destination*. The "prompt" sprite will then change to a blank costume since the move the complete.

Do you get the overall idea?

There is one point missing in the above discussion. How will the "prompt" sprite know when a rod was clicked by the user? And how will it know *which* rod was clicked?

Well, these are easier problems to solve. Basically, each rod will save its name in some global variable when it is clicked, and then send out a broadcast message.

Feature Idea # 6: Enforcing game rule #2

When the source and destination rods are selected (as above), the top disc from the "source" rod should move to the "destination" rod.

Step 1: Update the string ("L") variables of both rods appropriately.

Design:

As discussed earlier, the discs mounted on each rod are listed in its own local variable called "L". For example, when the game begins, L of sprite T1 contains "123" because all 3 discs are mounted on T1 and disc 3 is at the top.

To record the fact that the top disc has moved out, we just have to take the last digit from this string variable of the "source" rod and append it to the string variable of the "destination" rod.

For example, let's say, the user selects T1 as the source and T3 as the destination. This is how the lists should look before and after the move.

Before the move:
L of T1 = "123"
L of T3 = ""

After the move:
L of T1 = "12"
L of T3 = "3"

Let's say, after this move, the user once again selects T1 as the source and T3 as the destination. This is how the lists will look before and after the move.

Before the move:
L of T1 = "12"
L of T3 = "3"

After the move:
L of T1 = "1"
L of T3 = "32"

Do you get the idea?

How can we implement this in Scratch? Well, we can use the string operators (*join*, *letter*, and *length of*) for this purpose. Here are the steps you will need to follow:

Source rod will do this:

```
Get the last digit from its variable L.
Give it to the destination rod (via a variable).
Remove the last digit from L.
```

Destination rod will do this:
```
Append the digit to its variable L.
```

How would you get the last digit from L? Let's say L contains "123". Clearly we could use the command "letter 3 of L", where 3 is the length of the string. But, how do we get the length? We can use the operator "length of". The following combination operator will get the last digit of L:

Next, how do we *remove* the last letter from a string? Luckily, our string is always a number, so we can use an arithmetic operation to get rid of the last digit.

For example, to remove 3 from 123, we can divide 123 by 10 and ignore the remainder.

The following operator achieves this in Scratch:

Now, try to write your own scripts.

Step 2: *Move the disc from source to destination.*

Design:

Thus far, we have only manipulated variables; no disc has actually moved. The next task is to initiate a move. We already have scripts in each disc for the move. In the earlier version, the move was initiated by clicking on the disc. Now, we want to initiate it by sending a message. So, all we have to do is use the exact same script but change its event to "When message received".

As you know, the "prompt" script sets up the move by setting up the *source* and *destination* variables. It can then send out a message telling everyone that the move can proceed.

Each rod will receive this message and process it if it is the *source* rod. It will run the following steps:
```
Get the top disc number from "L".
```

Ask the disc to move.

Feature Idea # 7: Initial setup
Arrange discs properly on rod T1 when the game begins.

Design:
This task is straightforward. When the game begins we will ask all discs to first assemble in some corner of the screen. And then, they will be asked to stack up one by one on rod T1 in the order of their size. The stage can do the job of sending messages one by one.

Save as Program Version 2
Before continuing to the next set of ideas, we will save our project. This way, we have a backup of our project that we can go back to if required for any reason.

Compare your program with my program at the link below.

Hanoi-2: includes ideas 4 thru 7 explained above.
Link: https://scratch.mit.edu/projects/87302772/

How to run the program:
1. Click the "Green flag": a help screen appears. Read the instructions carefully.
2. Click anywhere to continue.
3. Press SPACEBAR to move one disc at a time.

Next Set of Features/ideas:
Next, we will try to enforce rule #3 of the game, that is, a disc will be allowed to move only if it is *smaller* than the top disc on the *destination* rod.

Presently, the user has to press SPACE BAR *every time* he/she wants to move a disc. We will make this automatic, i.e. the user will press SPACE BAR only once, and the program will repeatedly ask the user for the next move.

For this version, make a copy of your project (using "Save as") under a different name. For example, I am calling my copy as Hanoi-3.

Let us get cracking with these ideas and features one by one.

Feature Idea # 8: Enforce rule #3
Allow a disc to move only if it is smaller than the top disc on the destination rod.

Design:

We already have the required framework in place to implement this. We have variables called L that specify for each rod the existing stack of discs on that rod. We have a variable called *wannasend* that specifies which disc the user is trying to move. We have variables called *source* and *destination* which specify the source and target rods. And, the *source* rod informs the *destination* rod about the move by sending a "takeit" message.

So, all we need to do is have the *destination* rod do the following:
- Get the last digit from its L (which is its top disc)
- Compare this with *wannasend*: if *wannasend* is smaller, allow the move, otherwise disallow the move.

How can the destination rod *allow* or *disallow* the move? It really can't! But, it can set a *variable* to let everyone know if the move *should* be allowed or not.

See if you can modify your scripts to implement this idea.

Feature Idea # 9: Press SPACE BAR only once

Instead of having to press SPACE BAR for every disc move, require the user to do it only once. The program should then repeatedly ask for subsequent moves.

Design:

This may sound like a big change, but it is really quite easy to implement. As you know, the very first thing that happens (when the game begins) is that the user presses SPACE BAR. At that time, the "prompt" sprite changes its costume and asks the user to "Click on the source rod". So, the *change of costume* is what starts the process of moving a disc. All we have to do to make this process repetitive is to insert the "costume change" at the end of the disc move. This involves inserting just one command in the script of the "prompt" sprite.

Save as Program Version 3

Before continuing to the next set of ideas, we will save our project. This way, we have a backup of our project that we can go back to if required for any reason.

Compare your program with my program at the link below.

Hanoi-3: includes ideas 8 and 9 explained above.
Link: https://scratch.mit.edu/projects/87302598/

How to run the program:
1. Click the "Green flag": a help screen appears. Read the instructions carefully.
2. Click anywhere to continue.
3. Press SPACEBAR to start the disc moves.

Final Set of Features/ideas:
So far, we have been playing the game only with 3 discs. We will now look at allowing a variable number of discs (with some limit of course). We will also add a discouraging sound (!) when a wrong move is attempted by the user.

For this final version, make a copy of your project (using "Save as") under a different name. For example, I am calling my copy as Hanoi-final.

Let us get cracking with these ideas and features one by one.

Feature Idea # 10: Number of discs
Instead of having a fixed number of discs (3), allow the user choose the number of discs (from 1 to 5). This change will require several steps:
- *Allow the user to select the number of discs.*
- *Add a button called "Setup" that user will click, which will cause the following actions.*
  - ○ *Stacking up all discs on T1.*
  - ○ *Initializing the "L" variable of each rod appropriately.*
- *The user should not be able to play the game until all setup is done.*

Step 1: Allow the user to select the number of discs.

Design:
We will decide on a maximum number of discs (say 5) and have that many disc sprites ready (with decreasing size, of course). The next obvious thing to do is create a variable for the "number of discs". Let's call it *Discs*. To allow the user to set this variable at the start of the game, we will make it a *slider* variable with *minimum* and *maximum* set properly.

Step 2: Add a "Setup" button sprite as a remote control.

Design:
First, let's fully understand why this button is needed.

When the program starts, we will need to first allow the user to set the slider variable *Discs*, then set up the discs accordingly, and then start the game. In the earlier version of our program this wasn't necessary because the number of discs was fixed.

The best way to implement this multi-step start is to have an additional button called "Setup" that the user would click on after setting the slider variable. When "Setup" is clicked, it should send out a message to all those who have some setup work of their own.

Step 3: Stack up discs on T1 when "Setup" is clicked.

Design:
First of all, only those discs that are required in the game will show up for work. For example, if *Discs* is set to 2, only the two largest discs will become visible, and the rest will hide. Thus, every disc must run this check after "Setup" is clicked.

Secondly, our code to stack up discs on the leftmost rod (T1) will also need modification: it will use the *Discs* variable to decide how many discs to stack up.

Step 4: Initialize the "L" variable of each rod appropriately.

Design:
Earlier, we had a fixed number of discs (3), so it was straightforward to initialize the L variables. L of T1 was simply set to "123" and the rest of them were set to blank.

But, now this will depend on the *Discs* variable. The good news is, only T1's script will get affected since we are stacking up all discs on T1.

For example, if *Discs*=2, L (of T1) would be "12". If *Discs*=4, L would be "1234".

This can be accomplished by a simple loop that counts from 1 to *Discs*.

Step 5: Disallow the user from playing the game until all setup is done.

Design:
The user must not be allowed to start playing the game, i.e. start moving discs, until setup is complete. We can enforce this by using the concept of "using variables as gates". We will create a variable called *setupdone* which will be *False* initially and *True* after setup is done.

Feature Idea # 11: Sounds
When an illegal move is attempted, make a suitable sound.

Design:

Where in the program do we know that an illegal move was attempted? Well, it's in the script of each rod that processes the "canyoutakeit" message. Insert your sound there.

Save as the Final Program Version

Congratulations! You have completed all the main features of the game. As before, let's save this project before continuing to the advanced ideas.

Compare your program with my program at the link below.

Hanoi-final: includes ideas 10 and 11 explained above.
Link: `https://scratch.mit.edu/projects/87006602/`

How to run the program:
1. Click the "Green flag": a help screen appears. Read the instructions carefully.
2. Click anywhere to continue.
3. Using the "Discs" slider pick the number of discs: 1 to 5.
4. Click "Setup" to arrange the discs on one of the rods.
5. Press SPACE BAR to move the discs yourself, one disc at a time.

Advanced Set of Features/ideas:

The earlier version of our program only runs in the manual mode. That is, the user has to solve the puzzle. But, how about teaching the computer to solve the puzzle? That's what we will attempt in the advanced version.

For this advanced version, make a copy of your project (using "Save as") under a different name. For example, I am calling my copy as Hanoi-adv.

Feature Idea # 12: Solve the puzzle

Figure out a way in which the computer can solve the Tower of Hanoi puzzle. That is, at a click of button, the program should move (in slow motion) the stack of discs from one rod to another without, of course, violating the rules of the game.

Step 1: Include a "Solve" button which is for the computer to solve the puzzle.

Design:

Well, this is straightforward. Make this button become visible after setup is done. And if the user presses SPACE BAR – which means he/she wants to solve the puzzle himself/herself – make this button hide. And if the user clicks on this button, it should invoke the script that we will design in step 2 below.

Step 2: *Design a recursive script to solve the puzzle.*

Design:

Tower of Hanoi is an old and famous problem and mathematicians have invented several solutions for it. We will use the most popular *recursive solution* to this problem. This solution can be stated as follows:

To move N discs from rod T1 to rod T3:
- Move N−1 discs from T1 to T2. (This leaves the largest disc alone on T1).
- Move the remaining disc from T1 to T3.
- Move N−1 discs from T2 to T3.

If you read carefully, you will notice that steps 1 and 3 are identical to the original problem of moving a stack of ordered discs to another rod, except that the number of discs is smaller (by 1) than the original problem. This is exactly how recursion works: by reducing the original problem just slightly by adding a small and simple step, while retaining the overall flavor the problem.

Recursion in programming allows us to use a procedure to be called again and again. The above steps converted to an algorithm would look like the following:

```
MoveDiscs ( N, From, To, Spare )
        MoveDiscs( N-1,  From, Spare, To )
        MoveDiscs( 1,  From, To, Spare )
        MoveDiscs( N-1,  Spare, To, From )
```

Of course, this will not work because we will just keep calling the same procedure indefinitely. We must specify how the small step of moving 1 disc can be accomplished.

```
MoveDiscs( N, From, To, Spare )
        If (N = 1)
            Move one disc from "From" to "To"
        Else
            MoveDiscs( N-1,  From, Spare, To )
            MoveDiscs( 1,  From, To, Spare )
            MoveDiscs( N-1,  Spare, To, From )
        Endif
```

We already know how to move a single disc from one rod to another.

So, do you want to give this a try?

Feature Idea # 13: Speed of disc movement
As the number of discs increases, the computer would take longer to solve the puzzle. The main component of this time is spent in moving discs. Figure out a way to control the speed of the discs as they move from one rod to another.

Design:
If you study the script that moves a disc you will notice that the motion is conducted by *glide* commands. So, if we use a variable in the "time" input of each *glide*, we could control the speed of these glide commands.

Save as the Advanced Program Version
Congratulations! You have completed all the advanced features of the game. As before, let's save this project.

Compare your program with my program at the link below.

Hanoi-adv: includes idea 12 & 13 explained above.
Link: https://scratch.mit.edu/projects/87729932/

How to run the program:
1. Click the "Green flag": a help screen appears. Read the instructions carefully.
2. Click anywhere to continue.
3. Using the "Discs" slider pick the number of discs: 1 to 5.
4. Click "Setup" to arrange the discs on one of the rods.
5. Click "Solve" to make the computer solve the puzzle, or press SPACE BAR to move the discs yourself, one disc at a time.

Solutions to Feature Ideas

Feature idea # 1:
See the sprites in my program.

Feature idea # 2:

Step 1:

This command below will do the needful. Using the current "x position" ensures the disc only moves vertically. Y=40 is where the disc is well above each rod in my program. (It may be different in your program.)

Step 2:

As an example, this command below will move a disc to the destination rod T3. Using "y position" ensures that the disc only moves horizontally.

The complete script is shown in step 3.

Step 3:

The complete script for all 3 steps is shown below.

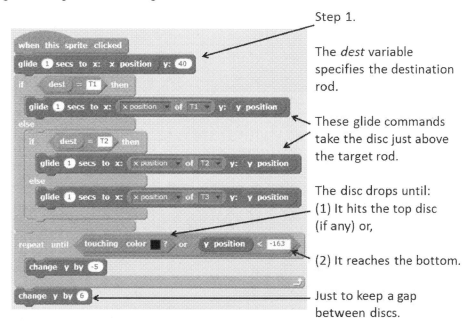

Step 1.

The *dest* variable specifies the destination rod.

These glide commands take the disc just above the target rod.

The disc drops until:
(1) It hits the top disc (if any) or,

(2) It reaches the bottom.

Just to keep a gap between discs.

In my program I have created a new command block called "Drop" to just do the dropping part in the above script.

Feature idea # 4:

Scripts to initialize the list variables: (Note that, in my program, I have named all 3 variables as L, because each of them is local and not visible to other sprites.)

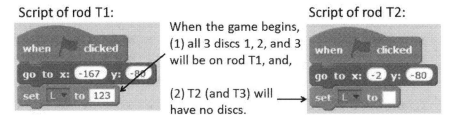

Script of rod T1:

Script of rod T2:

When the game begins, (1) all 3 discs 1, 2, and 3 will be on rod T1, and,

(2) T2 (and T3) will → have no discs.

Feature idea # 5:

Script for one of the rods (T1) to sense user click:

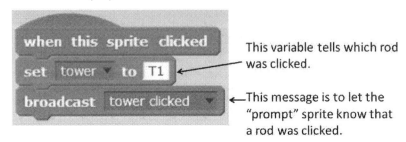

This variable tells which rod was clicked.

←This message is to let the "prompt" sprite know that a rod was clicked.

Scripts for the "prompt" sprite:

Initialization:

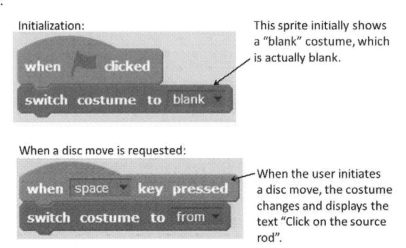

Initialization:

This sprite initially shows a "blank" costume, which is actually blank.

When a disc move is requested:

When the user initiates a disc move, the costume changes and displays the text "Click on the source rod".

When a rod is clicked it sends this message (this is the bulk of the work):

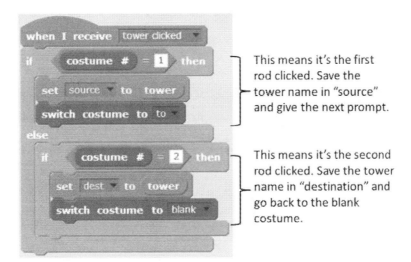

This means it's the first rod clicked. Save the tower name in "source" and give the next prompt.

This means it's the second rod clicked. Save the tower name in "destination" and go back to the blank costume.

Feature idea # 6:

First, we will modify the script of the "prompt" sprite slightly to include a broadcast message to indicate that the disc can be moved:

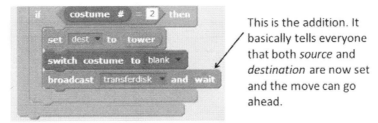

This is the addition. It basically tells everyone that both *source* and *destination* are now set and the move can go ahead.

This message will be received by each rod. The script for rod T1 is shown below:

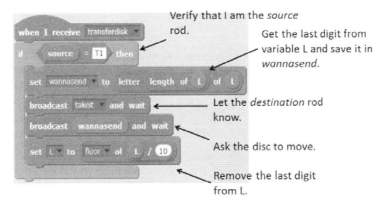

Verify that I am the *source* rod.

Get the last digit from variable L and save it in *wannasend*.

Let the *destination* rod know.

Ask the disc to move.

Remove the last digit from L.

Each rod will receive the "takeit" message. The script for rod T1 is shown below:

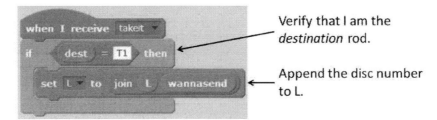

Verify that I am the *destination* rod.

Append the disc number to L.

Finally, the script of each disc is modified to accept a broadcast event instead of "When sprite clicked". This script below is for disc 1:

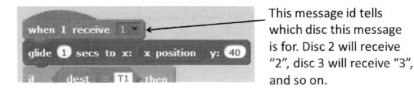

This message id tells which disc this message is for. Disc 2 will receive "2", disc 3 will receive "3", and so on.

Feature idea # 7:

Script for all disc sprites:

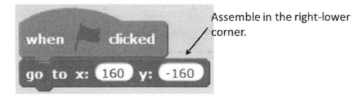

Assemble in the right-lower corner.

Stage sprite to arrange discs:

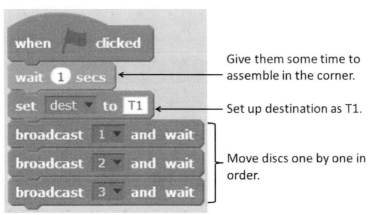

Give them some time to assemble in the corner.

Set up destination as T1.

Move discs one by one in order.

Feature idea # 8:

Modified script of each rod when it receives "transferdisc":

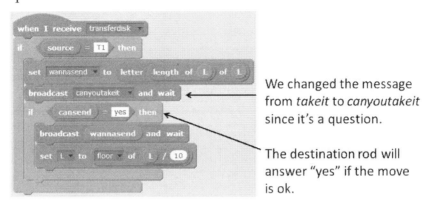

We changed the message from *takeit* to *canyoutakeit* since it's a question.

The destination rod will answer "yes" if the move is ok.

Modified script for each rod when it receives *canyoutakeit*:

Process message only if I am the *destination* rod.

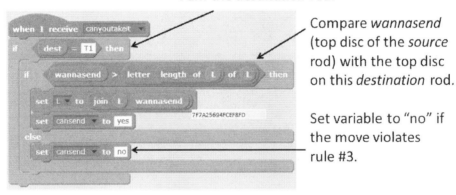

Compare *wannasend* (top disc of the *source* rod) with the top disc on this *destination* rod.

Set variable to "no" if the move violates rule #3.

Feature idea # 9:

Script for the "prompt" sprite which starts with "When I receive tower clicked":

This is the new addition. This does the job of setting up for the next disc move.

Feature idea # 10:

Step 1:

This just involves creating a slider variable (with min=1, max=5):

Step 2:

Scripts for the Setup button sprite:

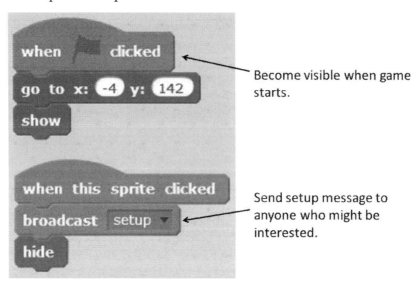

Become visible when game starts.

Send setup message to anyone who might be interested.

Step 3:

Script for disc 3:

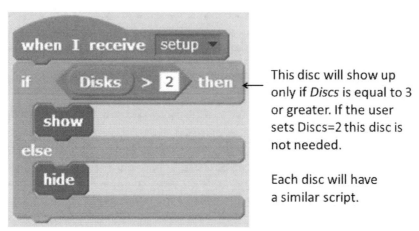

This disc will show up only if _Discs_ is equal to 3 or greater. If the user sets Discs=2 this disc is not needed.

Each disc will have a similar script.

Stage script for stacking up discs:

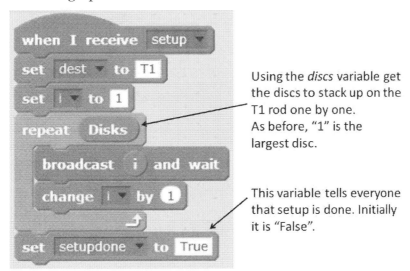

Using the *discs* variable get the discs to stack up on the T1 rod one by one. As before, "1" is the largest disc.

This variable tells everyone that setup is done. Initially it is "False".

Step 4:
Script for rod T1:

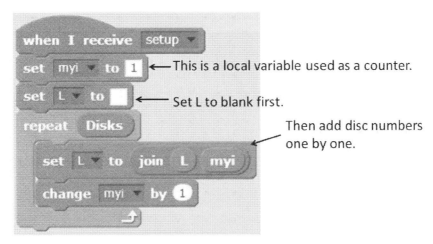

← This is a local variable used as a counter.

← Set L to blank first.

Then add disc numbers one by one.

Step 5:
Modified script of the "prompt" sprite:

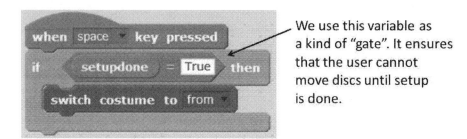

We use this variable as a kind of "gate". It ensures that the user cannot move discs until setup is done.

Feature idea # 11:
Check out my scripts in the program.

Feature idea # 12:
Script to invoke the recursive solution:

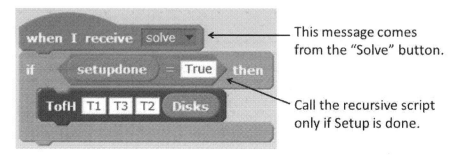

This message comes from the "Solve" button.

Call the recursive script only if Setup is done.

To see the recursive solution, just go to the program at the link given below.

Feature idea # 13:
Create a variable called *time* and use it in the time input of every *glide* command. Set it when the program starts.

The trouble with programmers is that you can never tell what a programmer is doing until it's too late. — Seymour Cray

Program Description

Connect Four is a 2-player game which consists of two sets of colored coins and a standing grid of rows and columns. Each player takes one set of coins and then by turn drops coins down any of the vertical columns (we will call them "tubes"). See the picture below.

The goal of the game is to get 4 coins of the same color to arrange themselves along a row, column, or diagonal. The first player to do this wins the game.

Do you want to check out a working Scratch version of this program? Click on the image below (or the URL just below it). I encourage you to explore the program and its various features. But, don't look at the Scratch scripts yet; we want to design this program ourselves!

How to run the program:

1. Click the "Green flag" to start the game.
2. Two users (blue and orange) will play the game by clicking alternately. The variable "Turn" shows whose turn it is.
3. Click the base of the tube in which you want to drop your coin.
4. Play until one of the players wins.

Link: https://scratch.mit.edu/projects/91400545/

Scratch and CS Concepts Used

When we design this program, we will make use of the following Scratch and CS concepts. I assume that you are already familiar with these concepts. If not, or if you want to brush up on these concepts, you should refer to the free downloadable supplement to this book at http://www.abhayjoshi.net/scratch/book1/supplement.pdf.

Main concepts:

- Algorithms
- Arithmetic operators (+, -, *, /)
- Arithmetic expressions
- Backdrops - multiple
- Conditionals (IF)
- Events
- Geometry - parallel lines
- Logic operators (and, or, not)
- Looping - simple (repeat, forever)
- Looping - conditional (repeat until)
- Motion - absolute
- Motion - smooth using repeat
- Pen commands
- Relational operators (=, <, >)
- Sensing touch
- Sequence

- Sounds - playing sounds
- STAMP - creating images
- Synchronization using broadcasting
- User events (mouse)
- Variables - numbers
- Variables - strings
- Variables - properties (built-in)
- XY Geometry

High Level Design:

This is where we take a step back from the computer (literally!), analyze the problem in our mind (and on a piece of paper if necessary), and break it down into multiple smaller ideas which can be programmed separately.

Let's take a look at the main screen of the game and try to point out the different pieces.

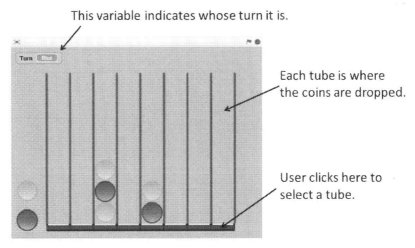

This variable indicates whose turn it is.

Each tube is where the coins are dropped.

User clicks here to select a tube.

Initial Set of Features:

Clearly it makes sense to start with the most basic apparatus – which is 2 sets of coins and the grid. At this stage, we *won't* trouble ourselves with the actual playing part or rules of the game (as listed in "program description" above). We will implement the game's main user interface and get all sprites in place. How will we represent the collection of coins? Once a coin is dropped in a tube, it doesn't do anything. So, we could use just 2 coin sprites and use the STAMP command to create images of the dropped coins. We also need a grid of identical tubes (columns) each with a solid clickable base.

That will be our starting version of the game. We will discuss what to do next after building this version.

For this initial version, give your project a special name (using "Save as"). For example, I am calling my copy as Connect4-1.

Let us get rolling with these various ideas one by one. Be sure to try writing your own scripts for each idea before looking up the "Solutions" section.

Feature Idea # 1: Coins and the grid
Draw the coin sprites and the grid of vertical tubes.

Step 1: Draw the coin sprites.

Design:
To play the game we need lots of orange and lots of blue coins. But, how many *sprites* do we need?

Let us consider what happens to each coin. When a coin is dropped into a tube it just sits there until the game is over. So, we don't really need an actual coin sprite in the tube; an image would suffice. Does that give you some idea?

Yes, we can use the STAMP command to create an image of a coin when it is dropped in a tube. So, that means we just need two sprites: one for the orange coin and one for the blue coin. We will take care of the actual script later. For now, we will just draw the sprites.

Draw circle sprites with thick border. Fill them with gradient of the same color. Resize them such that they fit the width of the tube.

Step 2: Draw the grid (series of tubes).

Design:
It is really up to us to decide how many tubes we should have. In my program, I have drawn 8 tubes. You can do the same or use a different number.

The grid, as you can see, has two parts:
1. A series of vertical lines which define the tubes

2. A solid base for each tube

The solid base of each tube will have to be a separate sprite, because, the players will select a tube by clicking its base. We can just draw one base and create duplicate sprites.

The vertical lines can be drawn as a sprite (or part of the background), but it is quite tedious to draw equidistant (equally spaced) parallel lines in the paint editor. Instead, we will draw them in the program itself using the Pen commands and some simple geometry. First, we will draw the 8 bottom sprites and line them up in a straight line (see solution below).

The algorithm to draw the lines for the tubes is quite simple. Let's say "w" is the width and "h" is the height of each tube. Let's say point (x, y) is on the left edge of the first base.

Algorithm to draw the tubes:

```
Go to x, y
Repeat 9
    Pen down
    Change y by h
    Pen up
    Change y by -h
    Change x by w
End-repeat
```

Save as Program Version 1

Before continuing to the next set of ideas, we will save our project. This way, we have a backup of our project that we can go back to if required for any reason.
Compare your program with my program at the link below.

Connect4-1: includes idea 1 explained above.
Link: https://scratch.mit.edu/projects/92038871/

How to run the program:
This program version doesn't do anything.

Next Set of Features/ideas:

Next, we will write scripts for dropping coins in the tubes. This involves the following features:

- choosing a tube
- choosing the right coin to drop
- positioning a coin on top of the selected tube
- dropping a coin down the selected tube

For this version, make a copy of your project (using "Save as") under a different name. For example, I am calling my copy as Connect4-2.

Let us get cracking with these ideas and features one by one.

Feature Idea # 2: Choosing tube and coin

Implement ways for the players to choose a tube, and to take turns.

Design:

Selecting a tube is straightforward. Since each tube has a separate base sprite, the players can simply click on the base to choose a tube.

To ensure players play by turn, we can have a variable called "Turn" which will indicate whose turn it is. If it says "orange" an orange coin will be dropped and if it says "Blue" a blue coin will be dropped.

Feature Idea # 3: Drop the coin

Write scripts to position the selected coin on top of the selected tube and drop it into the selected tube.

Step 1: Position the coin on top of the selected tube.

Design:

The variable "Turn" tells us which coin is to be dropped. The player will click on the base of the selected tube. In order to position a coin on top of this tube we need to know the X and Y co-ordinates of the point. We can pick some arbitrary value of Y which is somewhere above all tubes. How about X?

Well, we can use the X of the base sprite, right? Each base, when clicked, can save its X position in a variable.

Step 2: _Drop the coin into the selected tube._

Design:

Making the coin drop into the tube is straightforward. We can make it move downward until it touches the base or another coin.

As we discussed earlier, we don't need to leave the coin in the tube; we can leave its image. The STAMP command will come handy for that purpose.

Save as Program Version 2

Before continuing to the next set of ideas, we will save our project. This way, we have a backup of our project that we can go back to if required for any reason.

Compare your program with my program at the link below.

Connect4-2: includes ideas 2 and 3 explained above.

Link: `https://scratch.mit.edu/projects/92137476/`

How to run the program:

1. Click the "Green flag" to start the game.
2. Two users (blue and orange) will play the game by clicking alternately. The variable "Turn" shows whose turn it is.
3. Click the base of the tube in which you want to drop your coin.

Final Set of Features/ideas:

We really have all the important features of the game working now. We will just add a few more features to make the program more tidy, robust, and user-friendly. Here are the things we will consider in this version:

- When a tube becomes full, don't allow coins to drop in it.
- Add a welcome screen.
- Add a help screen and sounds.
- Add code that will automatically place the pipe bases in a neat row.

For this final version, make a copy of your project (using "Save as") under a different name. For example, I am calling my copy as Connect4-final.

Let us get cracking with these ideas and features one by one.

Feature Idea # 4: Tube full condition

When a tube becomes full, don't allow coins to drop in it.

Design:

There are different ways to implement this feature. For example, you could keep a count of the number of coins inside each tube in a list variable, and check that count every time a coin is dropped.

I am going to use a much simpler idea which is as follows: Just start dropping the coin. After it reaches the lowest point, check its Y position and if it is more than a certain value (a point where the tube would look full), cancel the subsequent steps (i.e. creating its image etc.).

Do you like the idea?

If you do, modify your scripts to implement this idea.

Feature Idea # 5: Welcome and Help Screens

Add a welcome screen, a help screen and suitable sounds.

Design:

This should be straightforward. We will arrange things such that the welcome screen appears when Green Flag is clicked and everything else is hidden at that time. After a short time (say 4 seconds) the game screen will appear.

The help screen will be optional – available when some key is pressed. It should go away when the mouse pointer is clicked anywhere.

What about sounds? Well, I have added one sound clip which plays every time a coin is dropped.

Feature Idea # 6: Placement of bases

Use a script to automatically place the bases in a neat row.

Design:

This is a matter of using the X-Y geometry and the "Go to x, y" command. Since all bases are at the same height, the Y position of all will be the same. Now, if you know the width of each base and the x position of the first base, can you calculate the x positions of the subsequent bases?

Here is the algorithm for these calculations:

```
Let x be the position of the first base.
Let w be the width of each base.
X position of the 2nd base = x + 1*w
X position of the 3rd base = x + 2*w
X position of the 4th base = x + 3*w
```

Do you get the idea? Now, since the sprites only move by themselves, each base will need to place itself when the Green Flag is clicked.

Save as the Final Program Version

Congratulations! You have completed the program with all the features we had planned. Save your program as "Connect4-final.sb2".

Compare your program with my program at the link below.

Connect4-final: includes ideas 4, 5, and 6 explained above.
Link: https://scratch.mit.edu/projects/91400545/

How to run the program:

1. Click the "Green flag" to start the game.
2. Two users (blue and orange) will play the game by clicking alternately. The variable "Turn" shows whose turn it is.
3. Click the base of the tube in which you want to drop your coin.

Additional challenge

If you are interested, work on this additional challenge.

For idea #4 above, implement this alternate technique: Keep a count of the number of coins in each tube, and check that count every time. When the count reaches the upper limit, disallow adding any more coins. You could use a list variable for these counts.

Solutions to Feature Ideas

Feature idea # 1:

Step 1:
See the sprites below:

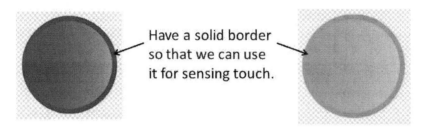

Have a solid border so that we can use it for sensing touch.

Step 2:
All 8 bases are lined up as shown below. Each of them is a separate sprite.

Refer to the program at the link below to check out the script to draw the tubes. You will need a separate sprite to do the drawing work. Any sprite will do!

Feature idea # 2:
Script for each base:

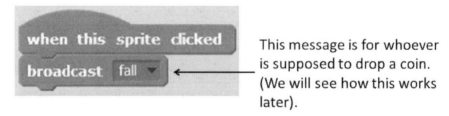

This message is for whoever is supposed to drop a coin. (We will see how this works later).

Feature idea # 3:

Step 1:

Modified script for each base:

Variable "tubex" would later be used by the coin to determine the X coordinate of the top point of the tube.

Script for the orange coin:

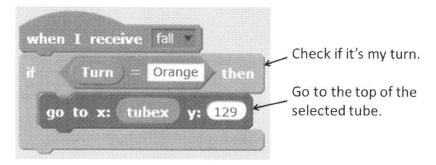

Check if it's my turn.

Go to the top of the selected tube.

Step 2:

Modified script for the orange coin:

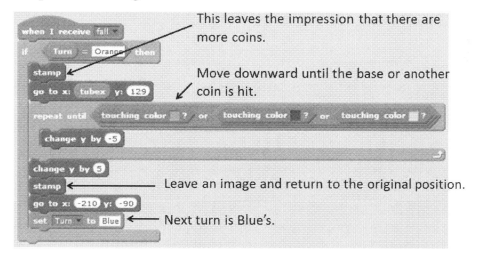

This leaves the impression that there are more coins.

Move downward until the base or another coin is hit.

Leave an image and return to the original position.

Next turn is Blue's.

Feature idea # 4:

Modified script of the "orange" coin:

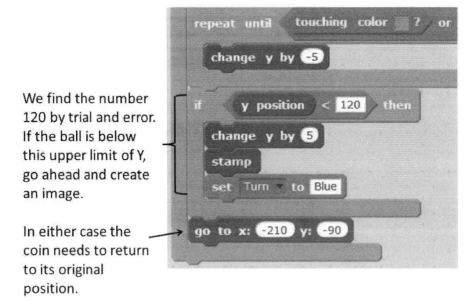

We find the number 120 by trial and error. If the ball is below this upper limit of Y, go ahead and create an image.

In either case the coin needs to return to its original position.

Feature idea # 6:

Script for base #2:

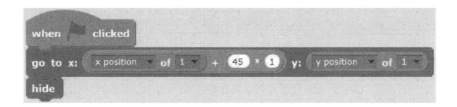

Script for base #4:

Project 10: Guess Arithmetic Operation

Game Description

This is a game in which you play to practice your arithmetic skill. A series of equations are shown on the screen and for each of them you need to guess the arithmetic operation. There are 4 buttons lined up marking the 4 operations: add, subtract, multiply, and divide. You need to click on the operation that fits the equation. For example, the equation could be: `10 ? 2 = 20`

You need to figure out which operation would fit in place of the question mark. In this case, it's the "multiply" operation.

The game has a timer of 30 seconds in which you try as many such equations as possible. When the timer expires, you get to see your score, and play again.

Do you want to check out a working Scratch version of this program? Click on the image below (or the URL just below it). I encourage you to explore the program and its various features. But, don't look at the Scratch scripts yet; we want to design this program ourselves!

How to play the game:

1. Click the "Green flag": you will see the welcome screen.
2. Press 'h' if you want to see game instructions.
3. Click START to start the game.
4. You have 30 seconds to do as many equations as possible.

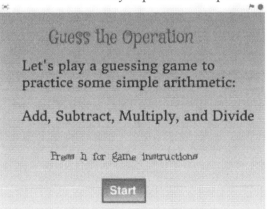

Link: https://scratch.mit.edu/projects/102812152/

Scratch and CS Concepts Used

When we design this program, we will make use of the following Scratch and CS concepts. I assume that you are already familiar with these concepts. If not, or if you want to brush up on these concepts, you should refer to the free downloadable supplement to this book at http://www.abhayjoshi.net/scratch/book1/supplement.pdf.

Main concepts:

-   Algorithms
-   Arithmetic operators (+, -, *, /)
-   Arithmetic expressions
-   Arithmetic operators (mod)
-   Backdrops - multiple
-   Concurrency - running scripts in parallel
-   Conditionals (If-Else)
-   Conditionals (IF)
-   Conditionals (Wait until)
-   Costumes
-   Events
-   Looping - simple (repeat, forever)
-   Looping - conditional (repeat until)
-   Random numbers
-   Random numbers - mapping to a set of things
-   Relational operators (=, <, >)
-   Sequence
-   STAMP - creating images
-   Stopping scripts
-   String operations
-   Synchronization using broadcasting
-   User events (keyboard)
-   User events (mouse)
-   User input (buttons)
-   Variables - numbers
-   Variables - as timer
-   XY Geometry

Additional concepts (for the advanced version):

-   Procedures with inputs

High Level Design:

Let's take a look at the main screen of the game and try to point out the different pieces.

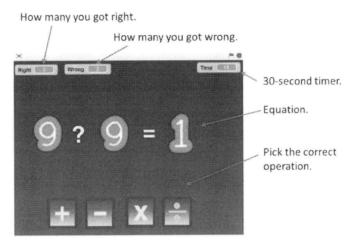

Let us consider the flow of operations in this program, which might give us some idea of the different parts that we need to design:

- Wait until user clicks "start".
- Timer starts.
- Two numbers *first* and *second* are selected randomly. An operation is picked randomly, and *result* is calculated. Numbers *first* and *second* will be single digit and so, result can be single or double-digit.
- The equation is displayed in the form *first ? second = result*.
- The 4 buttons for the 4 operations appear. The user clicks one of them.
- Program counts *right* or *wrong*.
- The next equation appears.
- After timeout the program stops.

The order in which we should work on these different pieces of the program is really up to us. It probably makes sense to first figure out how to display an arithmetic equation. We will design the required sprites and work out a way to display numbers. We will restrict to single digit numbers on the left-hand side of the equation and so, the resulting number on the right side can be single digit or double digit (9 x 9 = 81 is the largest possible result).

In the next version, we will tackle the challenge of displaying random equations and keeping score based on the operation clicked by the user.

In the final version, we will add niceties such as the timer, a start button, and welcome/help screens.

So, let's get rolling with these various ideas one by one. Be sure to try writing your own scripts for each idea before looking up the "Solutions" section.

Initial Version

In the initial version of the program, we will work on the following feature ideas:

1. Showing a single digit number on the screen.
2. Showing a 2-digit number on the screen.
3. Showing an arithmetic equation (just with the "+" operation) on the screen.
4. Showing the 4 buttons.

For this initial version, give your project a special name (using "Save as"). For example, I am calling my copy as Guess-operation-1.

Feature Idea # 1: Showing equations

Figure out a way to display a full equation on the screen: single digit numbers on the left side and 1 or 2-digit numbers on the right side, and the symbols "?" and "=".

We will break this work into multiple steps.

Step 1: Display the single digit numbers on the left-hand side of each equation.

Design:

A number consists of digits from 0 to 9. How do you think we can display single-digit numbers?

Well, one way to show a digit on the screen is to have a sprite with 10 costumes (each showing a digit 0 thru 9) and then use the "stamp" command to display a digit. So, depending on which digit we want to show, the sprite will switch to that costume and stamp it on the screen.

We will use variables *first* and *second* to store the numbers on the left-hand side of each equation. They will always be single-digit as we have decided. And, we will use a sprite called *digit* which will have 10 costumes – each showing a digit from 0 thru 9.

We will name these costumes as "0-glow", "1-glow", thru "9-glow" so that figuring out which costume maps to which number would be easy. "glow" is just my addition; you may use any word there.

<u>Note</u>: We can't name the costumes simply "0", "1", etc. because then, for example, "switch to costume 5" command would interpret 5 as the fifth costume in the list of costumes, and NOT the costume whose name is "5". Do you get it?

Now, let's take a concrete example: *first* = 5 and *second* = 7. How will we display these numbers?

The following algorithm shows how the *digit* sprite will show these digits.

```
Clear screen
Go to x y of "first"                          This is a convenient
Change to costume join first "-glow"  ←—— trick. If first = 5, the
Stamp                                         sprite will switch to
Go to x y of "second"                         costume "5-glow".
Change to costume join second "-glow"
Stamp
```

That wasn't too hard, was it?

<u>*Step 2*</u>: *Display the number on the right-hand side of each equation, which may be single digit or double digit.*

Design:

We will store the number on the right-hand side of each equation in a variable called *result*. For now, we will assume that the operation is always "+".

So, *result = first + second*

If *result* is single-digit (i.e. *result* < 10) we already know how to show it (as in step 1).

What will you do if *result* is double-digit (i.e. *result* > 9)? Let's use the example of 25. We will need to show digits 2 and 5 next to each other. But, how do we extract these digits from the number 25? Do you know any arithmetic tricks that we can use?

<u>Hint</u>: The "mod" operator gives the remainder of a division.

Here is how you can do it: 25 mod 10 will give 5 (the rightmost digit). Subtracting 5 from 25 will give 20. And finally 20 mod 10 will give 2 (the leftmost digit of 25).

The following algorithm shows how to extract the digits. Let's assume we have a temporary variable called *Temp*.

```
If result > 9
   Temp = (result - (result mod 10)) / 10        If result = 25,
                                                   this step will give 2.
   Show Temp as a single digit (step 1)
   Temp = result mod 10                            And this step will
   Show Temp as a single digit (step 1)           give 5.
Else
   Show result as a single digit (step 1)
End-if
```

Step 3: *Display different numbers each time the green flag is clicked.*

Design:

This is simply a matter of generating random numbers. Our left-hand numbers, i.e. *first* and *second* will be single digit and so we will pick from 0 to 9.

We can have the stage own this script which will generate the numbers and then send a broadcast message to the *digit* and other sprites to actually form an equation.

Feature Idea # 2: Buttons
Show the 4 arithmetic operations as buttons that user can click.

Design:

At this time, we are simply showing these buttons and not really taking any action if user clicks on them. So, we just need to create these sprites.

Save as Program Version 1

Before continuing to the next set of ideas, we will save our project. This way, we have a backup of our project that we can go back to if required for any reason.

Compare your program with my program at the link below.

Guess-operation-1: includes ideas 1 and 2 explained above.
Link: https://scratch.mit.edu/projects/102810767/

How to play the game:
1. Click the "Green flag" to see a new equation every time.

Next Set of Features/ideas:
1. Right now we show a new equation each time the green flag is clicked. Instead, as in the actual game, show a new equation only after user clicks one of the buttons.

2. Validate the clicked button and keep track of "right" and "wrong" answers.
3. Right now we just have the "+" operation in every new equation. Allow any of the four arithmetic operations: +. - , x, /

For this version, make a copy of your project (using "Save as") under a different name. For example, I am calling my copy as Guess-operation-2.

Feature Idea # 3: Series of equations

Right now we show a new equation each time the green flag is clicked. Instead, as in the actual game, show a new equation only after user clicks one of the buttons.

Design:

Creating a new equation involves two steps: (a) setting the variables and (b) sending the message *showdigits* which causes the equation and the buttons to appear.

Right now this is done by "stage" when green flag is clicked. If we want new equations to appear one after the other, we will need some kind of "looping" mechanism. Do you agree?

Let's just write down what we want:

```
Forever:
  Generate a new equation
  Wait till the user clicks one of the buttons
```

We will worry about how to terminate this loop (when the timer expires) later.

Now, how will you implement step 1 of this loop?

Well, we already have a script (in stage) that generates a new equation. That script can be invoked through a broadcast message from the forever loop.

How about step 2? What Scratch trick can you use?

Well, we can use a variable whose value will signal when a button has been clicked.

Feature Idea # 4: Track score

Validate the clicked button and keep track of "right" and "wrong" answers.

Design:

Clearly, we will need to use two more variables – *right* and *wrong* – to keep track of user responses. When the user clicks a button, the button script should check if the corresponding operation fits the given equation and increment the appropriate variable.

For example, if the equation is 5 ? 6 = 30, and if the user clicks the "+" (add) button, the script for "+" will check if 5 + 6 equals 30, and then, increment *wrong* because obviously 5+6 does not equal 30.

Write scripts for each button to implement this idea.

Feature Idea # 5: All operations
Right now we just have the "+" operation in every new equation. Allow any of the four arithmetic operations. Also make sure the numbers in the equation are properly calculated to fit each operation.

Let's do this work in multiple steps.

Step 1: Instead of having "+" every time, devise a mechanism to pick an operation at random.

Design:
We need to pick one of four operations. We know how to pick a random number from 1 to 4. How do we use that idea to select an arithmetic operation?

Well, we could *map* each number (from 1 to 4) to an arithmetic operation. For example, 1 would map to "+", 2 would map to "−", and so on. The subsequent design steps below will show how this mapping can be done.

For now, just write the script to pick a random number.

Step 2: Map the number 1 to the "+" operation.

Design:
We will map number 1 to the add operation, i.e. if "pick random" returns 1 we will consider that as the add operation.

We are using variables *first* and *second* to denote the numbers on the left side of the equation. With the "+" operation, the *result* would be *first + second*.

Modify your script to implement this idea.

Step 3: Map the number 2 to the "−" operation.

Design:
We will map number 2 to the subtract operation, i.e. if "pick random" returns 2 we will consider that as the subtract operation.

For the subtract operation, the result would be *first – second*.

But, there is a small catch here. Do you see it?

We don't want to use negative numbers in this game. So, what should we do if *first* is smaller than *second*?

Well, we will simply swap them in that case.

See if you can update your script to implement this idea.

Step 4: Map the number 3 to the "x" operation.

Design:
We will map number 3 to the multiply operation, i.e. if "pick random" returns 3 we will consider that as the multiply operation.

For the multiply operation, the result would be *first* x *second*.

Update your script to implement this idea.

Step 5: Map the number 4 to the divide operation.

Design:
We will map number 4 to the divide operation, i.e. if "pick random" returns 4 we will consider that as the divide operation.

For the divide operation, the result would be *first / second*. But, there are a number of issues we must deal with:
1. First of all, *second* cannot be 0 because "divide by 0" is illegal.
2. Secondly, we only want whole numbers as result. For example, 5/2 won't be acceptable because the result would be 2.5.

How will you deal with these issues?

Well, to fix #1, we will pick *second* from 1 to 9 instead of 0 to 9. That is straightforward.

For #2, we will need to adjust *first* and *second* such that *result* is always a whole number. Can you figure out how to do this using your knowledge of arithmetic?

Well, we can modify *first* by looking at the value of *second*. For example, if *second* is 4, *first* can only be 0, 4, or 8 so that we get a whole number as division. This is really a matter of using the "multiply" operation to ensure we get a whole division.

See the algorithm below:

```
If second > 4                    If second is any of (5, 6, 7, 8, 9),
   first = second  ←─────────    this is the only way we can get
end-if                           a whole result.
If second = 4
   first = 4 x random(0,2)←──  If second = 4, first can be 0, 4, or 8.
end-if
If second = 3                    If second = 3, first can be
   first = 3 x random(0,3)←──  0, 3, 6, or 9.
end-if
If second = 2                    If second = 2, first can be
   first = 2 x random(0,4)←──  0, 2, 4, 6, or 8.
end-if
If second = 1
   first = random(0,9) ←──────  If second = 1, first can be any of
end-if                           0 to 9.
```

Update your script to include this idea.

Save as Program Version 2

Before continuing to the next set of ideas, we will save our project. This way, we have a backup of our project that we can go back to if required for any reason.

Compare your program with my program at the link below.

Guess-operation-2: includes ideas 3, 4, and 5 explained above.
Link: https://scratch.mit.edu/projects/102805001/

How to play the game:
1. Click the "Green flag" to start the game.
2. Click one of the 4 buttons. "Right" and "Wrong" will track your answers.
3. A new equation will appear after every button click. Play as long as you wish.

Final Set of Features/ideas:

Add a game timer and other niceties such as the *welcome* and *help* screens, a "Start" button, and a "Play again" button when timeout occurs.

For this final version, make a copy of your project (using "Save as") under a different name. For example, I am calling my copy as Guess-operation-final.

Feature Idea # 6: Welcome and Help
Add a welcome screen and also a help screen.

Design:
With the welcome screen we will also need a way to start the game, for which we will add a "Start" button. Let's do all this in steps:

Step 1: *Add a welcome screen.*

Design:

We will design a new sprite which will be as big as the whole screen and with appropriate welcome text. This sprite will appear when the Green flag is clicked. Obviously all other sprites (and variables) will need to hide while this screen is up.

Step 2: *Add a "Start" button.*

Design:

This button will also appear along with the welcome screen, and when it is clicked it will send a "begin" message so that the actual game screen and all other sprites (and variables) will appear. Earlier, the stage script that displays equations ran when the green flag was clicked; now it will run when the "begin" message is received.

Step 3: *Add a "help" screen.*

Design:

The help screen can be another costume of the "welcome" sprite and it will show up when the user pushes the "h" button.

Design your welcome/help screens and the start button.

Feature Idea # 7: Game timer and Play again

Include a count-down timer for the game and a "play again" button after timeout.

Design:

How will you count time?

We will do that using the "wait" command and our own variable called *timer*. We can add a script to the stage to count time and inform everyone when time is up.

When the *timer* value reaches 0, the game will be stopped and the user will be asked to check his/her score. In addition, we will provide a button called "Play again" if the user wants to play the game again.

Save as Program Version "Final"

Congratulations! You have completed all the main features of the game. As before, let's save this project before continuing to the advanced ideas.

Compare your program with my program at the link below.

Guess-operation-final: includes ideas 6 and 7 explained above.
Link: https://scratch.mit.edu/projects/102812152/

How to play the game:
1. Click the "Green flag": you will see the welcome screen.
2. Press 'h' if you want to see game instructions.
3. Click START to start the game.
4. You have 30 seconds to do as many equations as possible.
5. Click "Play again" after timeout, if you wish to play again.

Design Steps – Advanced Version

You can make several improvements to your program, one of which is listed below. This feature is optional, so, implement only if you find it interesting and useful.

For this advanced version, make a copy of your project (using "Save as") under a different name. For example, I am calling my copy as Guess-operation-adv.

Feature Idea # 8: Procedure for displaying digit

If you review feature idea #1, you will see that the script of the "digit" sprite contains code for displaying a digit which is repeated a number of times. You can make this script compact by writing a procedure to encapsulate this oft-used code.

Design:
The code that displays number *first* (which is a single digit) is as follows:

Similar code is used for *second* and then for the two digits of *result*.

We can't just make these lines into a procedure, because several things change: for example, the numbers used in the "Go to" command. In order to put these 3 lines into a procedure, we need to figure out which parts will become *inputs* of the procedure. What do you think?

Below, I show the script again pointing out the inputs.

Both x and y will be inputs, and so will the first part of join.

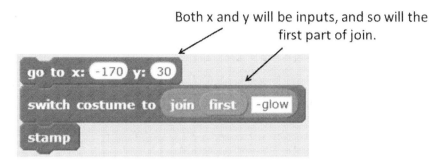

Go ahead, write this procedure yourself and then call it from the script of the sprite *digit*.

Save as Program Version "Advanced"

Congratulations! You have completed all the advanced features of the game. As before, let's save this project.

Compare your program with my program at the link below.

Guess-operation-adv: includes the advanced features listed above.
Link: https://scratch.mit.edu/projects/102805218/

How to play the game:

1. Click the "Green flag": you will see the welcome screen.
2. Press 'h' if you want to see game instructions.
3. Click START to start the game.
4. You have 30 seconds to do as many equations as possible.
5. Click "Play again" after timeout, if you wish to play again.

Additional Challenge(s)

Add some interesting sounds to your program so that the user will get an audio indication when the answer is right and when it is wrong.

Solutions to Feature Ideas

Feature idea # 1:
Step 1:
Script for the "digit" sprite:

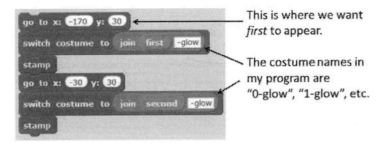

This is where we want *first* to appear.

The costume names in my program are "0-glow", "1-glow", etc.

Step 2:

Script for the "digit" sprite for result of each equation:

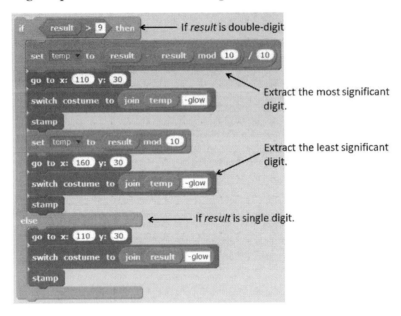

If *result* is double-digit

Extract the most significant digit.

Extract the least significant digit.

If *result* is single digit.

Step 3:

Script owned by "stage":

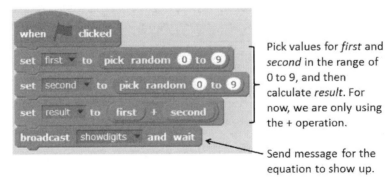

Pick values for *first* and *second* in the range of 0 to 9, and then calculate *result*. For now, we are only using the + operation.

Send message for the equation to show up.

Feature idea # 2:

Button sprites for the arithmetic operations:

Feature idea # 3:

Script for the "stage":

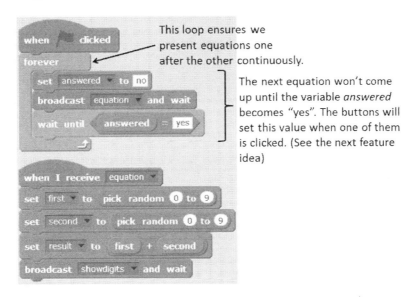

This loop ensures we present equations one after the other continuously.

The next equation won't come up until the variable *answered* becomes "yes". The buttons will set this value when one of them is clicked. (See the next feature idea)

Feature idea # 4:

Script for the "multiply" sprite:

Run the equation for the "*" operator and See if you get the desired result.

This will unblock the "wait until" command in the Forever loop.

Feature idea # 5:

Step 1:

Command to pick an operation:

Step 2:

Snippet of the script that creates an operation:

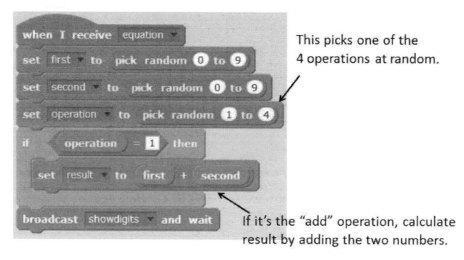

This picks one of the 4 operations at random.

If it's the "add" operation, calculate result by adding the two numbers.

Step 3:

Calculation for the subtract operation:

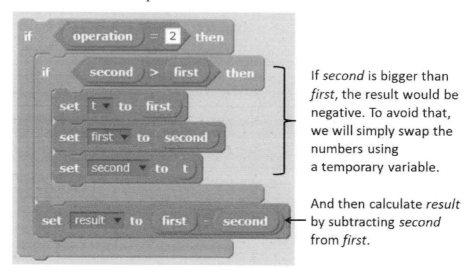

If *second* is bigger than *first*, the result would be negative. To avoid that, we will simply swap the numbers using a temporary variable.

And then calculate *result* by subtracting *second* from *first*.

<u>*Step 4*</u>:

Calculation for the multiply operation:

<u>*Step 5*</u>:

Calculation for the divide operation:

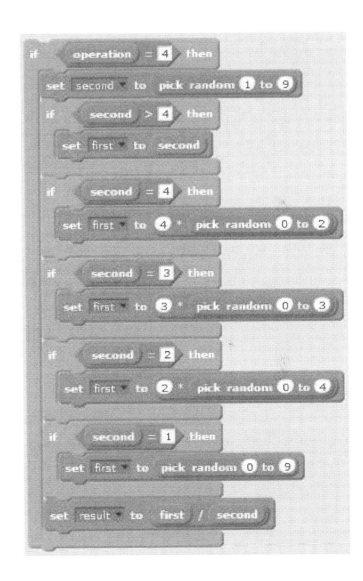

Feature idea # 6:

Script for the "start" button:

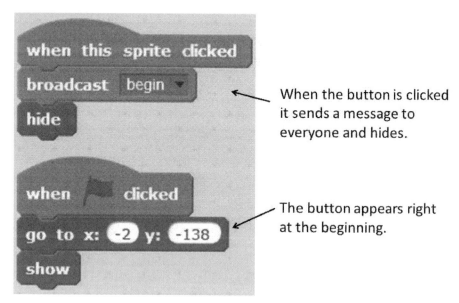

When the button is clicked it sends a message to everyone and hides.

The button appears right at the beginning.

All other sprites will have these additional scripts:

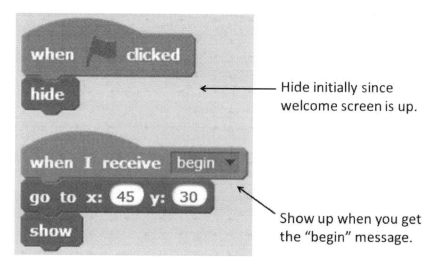

Hide initially since welcome screen is up.

Show up when you get the "begin" message.

Feature idea # 7:

Script for the timer:

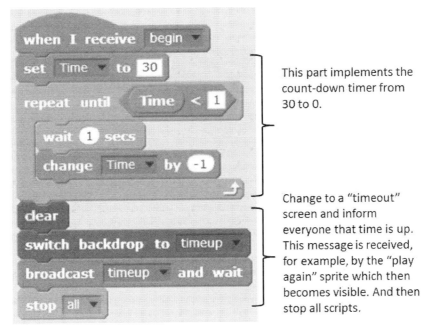

This part implements the count-down timer from 30 to 0.

Change to a "timeout" screen and inform everyone that time is up. This message is received, for example, by the "play again" sprite which then becomes visible. And then stop all scripts.

Scripts for the "play again" button:

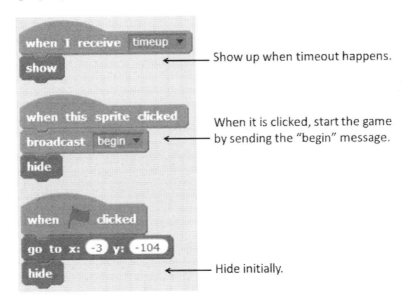

Show up when timeout happens.

When it is clicked, start the game by sending the "begin" message.

Hide initially.

Feature idea # 8:

Procedure "ShowDigit":

And here is the modified compact script for the *digit* sprite:

```
when I receive showdigits
clear
ShowDigit -170 30 first
ShowDigit -30 30 second
if  result > 9  then
    ShowDigit 110 30  result - result mod 10 / 10
    ShowDigit 160 30  result mod 10
else
    ShowDigit 110 30  result
```

Appendix

Required CS and Scratch Concepts

The projects covered in this book are all based on a variety of CS and Scratch concepts. The book does not attempt to explain these concepts. But, I have prepared a supplement that provides a brief description of each of these concepts. I assume that you are already familiar with these concepts. If not, or if you want to brush up on them, refer to the brief description of each concept provided in this supplement. It is NOT a rigorous and comprehensive explanation of concepts, but only a quick summary.

This supplement is available for a free download at:

http://www.abhayjoshi.net/scratch/book1/supplement.pdf

These concepts are also fully explained with programming examples and projects in my other Scratch programming book **Learn CS Concepts with Scratch** which is available both in digital and print format on Amazon.com. Look up the following for more information on this book:

http://www.abhayjoshi.net/mybooks/bscratch.pdf

Printed in Great Britain
by Amazon